# MOUNTAIN
# RESCUE TECHNIQUES

## WASTL MARINER

*Drawings by Fritz and Gert Ebster*
*First Aid Instructions by Dr. med. Hans Heinz Seidel,*
*revised by Otto T. Trott, M.D. and Kurt G. Beam,*
*First Aid Instructor, American Red Cross*

*Oesterreichischer Alpenverein, Innsbruck, Wilhelm-Greil-Str. 15*
*Distributed in North America by The Mountaineers*
*P. O. Box 122 Seattle, Washington, 98111*

Printed by Frohnweiler, Innsbruck, Maria-Theresien-Strasse 40, Austria

# OESTERREICHISCHER ALPENVEREIN

## AUSTRIAN ALPINE ASSOCIATION

### FOUNDED IN 1862

---

*Cover drawing: Emblem of Mountain Rescue Association of North America*

---

*First Edition, 1948*          *Second Edition, 1959*

*First English-Language Edition, 1963*

# FOREWORD
## to the Second German=Language Edition

The original edition of this manual, published in 1948, carried a foreword by our honorary member, Hofrat Martin Busch, first President of the Oesterreichischer Alpenverein and for many years Chairman of its Board of Directors. In that foreword he said: "Mountaineering technique and equipment of today are considerably different from that of 80, 40, or 20 years ago; no less changed are the technique and equipment of modern mountain rescues."

Appropriate as his remark was then, it is even more so now. Advances in rescue methods from the early days of mountaineering through 1948 were great; those since 1948 can only be called revolutionary.

The pioneers of this new age of rescue have been, in the main, members of the Oesterreichischer Alpenverein working in partnership with their comrades in the Deutscher Alpenverein. Sponsored and subsidized by these organizations, they have evolved a technique literally beyond the imagination of earlier generations. That technique, developed by a few, is here presented to the many, to become the common property of the entire mountain world.

The rudiments of organized mountain rescue in the Eastern Alps date from 1896 in Vienna, and from 1898 in Graz, Salzburg, and Innsbruck. Since those early days, the Alpenverein has steadily advocated improved methods and organization, feeling it could not encourage the sport of alpinism without preparing, in advance, for alpine misfortunes.

The first edition of this manual, though published in large quantity, has long been out of print — a good sign of its merits. A further indication of need has been the large number of translations of that edition, authorized and otherwise. However, despite continuing demand, we have not reprinted the original edition lest we thereby perpetuate methods which were once the best available, but have since been superseded. We are at last ready to publish the new methods, certain that their technical refinement is such that they will not be radically modified in the near future. To be sure, rescue teams will find radios and helicopters increasingly important, but it would be a grave mistake to depend excessively on modern technology so long as mountaineering resembles the sport we know today. The most important factor in mountain rescue will continue to be the skilled mountaineer who is prepared to risk his life in the stormswept high reaches of the world.

The best way to reduce the need for organized rescue services is to train every mountaineer in rescue methods. Thus he learns how to help both himself and others. Thus, also, he learns the consequences of an accident and learns to treat the mountains with proper respect. We urge, therefore, that this manual be made available through all rescue organizations and mountaineering clubs. Every member of a rescue team should carry a copy in his personal kit. Since every mountaineer on every climb is at every moment a potential rescuer, he should own a copy and be familiar with its contents.

For the sake of wide distribution, we have produced this manual as inexpensively as possible, with no thought of profit. In this, we have followed the example of the author, who has refused to accept any fee. Here we would like to express, on behalf of all mountaineers everywhere, our profound gratitude to the author for taking as great pains with this second edition as he did with the first. No one else had equal qualifications for the task; his has been a central role in pioneering the new age of rescue.

*Mountain Rescue Techniques* now ventures forth a second time, once more carrying the sincere hope of the Oesterreichischer Alpenverein that it will aid the humanitarian efforts of rescue teams throughout the mountain world.

**Hans Kinzl**

First President

Oesterreichischer Alpenverein

# FOREWORD
# to the English=Language Edition

There are many mountain ranges, but there is a single mountain world. All mountaineers, wherever they live and climb and whatever language they speak, share common citizenship.

The Mountain Rescue Council, organized in 1948 under the leadership of Wolf Bauer, has followed closely the creation and evolution of the rescue methods described in this manual. The Council feels honored, now, to help make these methods available to others, and so to repay, in part, a debt of gratitude to Wastl Mariner and the Oesterreichischer Alpenverein. The Council also takes this opportunity to acknowledge with thanks the friendly cooperation and assistance offered during its early years by Dr. med. Rometsch and the Bergwacht of the Bavarian Red Cross.

The translation has been carried out by Otto T. Trott M. D. and Kurt G. Beam, both members of the Mountain Rescue Council, The Mountaineers, The American Alpine Club, and the National Ski Patrol. While taking idiomatic liberties for the sake of clarity, they have adhered as closely as possible to the German text in order to guarantee accurate transmission of Wastl Mariner's ideas. The first aid instructions, however, have been considerably modified and enlarged in the light of recent medical knowledge; in this the translators were greatly helped by the comments offered by Dr. med. Rudolf Campell of Switzerland, President of the International Commission for Alpine Rescue (IKAR), and Benjamin G. Ferris Jr. M.D., Chairman of the Safety Committee of the American Alpine Club. The translation was edited by Harvey Manning (The Mountaineers), Howard Miller (The Mountaineers), and Murrell Boyd, aided by Laine Henline (The Mountaineers) as manuscript typist and coordinator.

The Oesterreichischer Alpenverein initiated this translation in the hope that English-speaking mountainclimbers might find the modern rescue methods as useful as have their German-speaking comrades. To that hope, we now add our own.

**The Mountain Rescue Council**
Seattle, Washington, U. S. A.
1 9 6 3

# Mountain Rescue Groups

## Mountain Rescue Groups in North America

*Indicates Membership in the Mountain Rescue Association*

| Group | Location | Area Covered |
|---|---|---|
| Mountain Rescue Association (coordinating group) | P.O. Box 67 Seattle, Washington 98111 | |
| **ALASKA** | | |
| *Alaska Rescue Group, Inc. | Anchorage, Alaska | All of Alaska |
| Alpine Rescue Unit of Alaska | Fairbanks, Alaska | N. E. Alaska Range and Brooks Range |
| **ALBERTA, CANADA** | | |
| Banff National Park Rescue Service | Banff National Park Banff, Alberta | Canadian Rockies |
| **ARIZONA** | | |
| *Southern Arizona Rescue Association | Tuscon, Arizona | Arizona |
| **BRITISH COLUMBIA, CANADA** | | |
| *Mountain Rescue Group | Vancouver, B.C. | Coast Range and North Cascades |
| **CALIFORNIA** | | |
| *Altadena Mountain Rescue Squad | Altadena, California | Los Angeles County and environs |
| *China Lake Mountain Rescue Group | China Lake, California | Southern Sierra Range and Eastern flank of Sierra Range |
| *Riverside Mountain Rescue Unit | San Jacinto, California | San Jacinto Mountains |
| Montrose Mountain Search and Rescue Unit | Montrose, California | Montrose Area |

| Group | Location | Area Covered |
|---|---|---|
| *San Gorgonio Search and Rescue | Redlands, California | San Bernardino Mountains |
| Sierra Club; Mountain Rescue Committee | Berkeley, California | Yosemite and environs |
| *Sierra Madre Search and Rescue Team | Sierra Madre, California | Sierra Madre Mountains and Los Angeles County |

## COLORADO

| | | |
|---|---|---|
| *Alpine Rescue Team | Arvada, Colorado | Colorado Rockies |
| Fort Carson NCO Academy Mountain Rescue Group | Colorado Springs, Colorado | Colorado Rockies |
| *Rocky Mountain Rescue Group, Inc. | Boulder, Colorado | Colorado Rockies |

## IDAHO

| | | |
|---|---|---|
| *Idaho Mountain Search and Rescue Unit | Boise, Idaho | Idaho |

## MONTANA

| | | |
|---|---|---|
| *Missoula Mountain Rescue Unit | Missoula, Montana | Western Montana and Northern Idaho |

## NEW HAMPSHIRE

| | | |
|---|---|---|
| Appalachian Mountain Club | Pinkham Notch, New Hampshire | White Mountains |

## NEW MEXICO

| | | |
|---|---|---|
| Rescue Group | Albuquerque, New Mexico | New Mexico |
| Rescue Group; Southwestern Mountaineers | Las Cruce, New Mexico | Southern New Mexico and Western tip of Texas |

| Group | Location | Area Covered |
|---|---|---|
| **OREGON** | | |
| *Mountain Rescue and Safety Council of Oregon (MRSCO) | Portland 7, Oregon | Oregon and Southern Washington |
| *Alpinees, Inc. | Hood River, Oregon | Oregon and Southern Washington |
| *Corvallis Unit MRSCO Club | Corvallis, Oregon | Oregon and Southern Washington |
| *Crag Rats | Hood River, Oregon | Oregon and Southern Washington |
| *Eugene Unit MRSCO | Eugene, Oregon | Oregon and Southern Washington |
| *Salem Unit MRSCO | Salem, Oregon | Oregon and Southern Washington |
| **QUEBEC, CANADA** | | |
| Montreal Mountain Rescue Group | Pointe Claire P.Q. | Quebec, Northern New York, New Hampshire, Vermont, Maine |
| **VERMONT** | | |
| *Mad River Mountain Rescue Unit | Waitsfield, Vermont | Vermont |
| Mountain Rescue Group | Norwich University Northfield, Vermont | Northern New Hampshire and Vermont |
| **WASHINGTON** | | |
| *Bellingham Mountain Rescue Council | Bellingham, Washington | Northern Cascades |
| Central Washington Mountain Rescue Council | Yakima, Washington | East Central Cascades |
| *Everett Mountain Rescue Unit, Inc. | Everett, Washington | Cascade Range |
| Mt. St. Helens Rescue Unit | Longview, Washington | Mt. St. Helens |

11

| Group | Location | Area Covered |
|---|---|---|
| *Olympic Mountain Rescue Council | Bremerton, Washington | Olympic Range |
| *Paine Field Search and Rescue Team | Paine Field Everett, Washington | North Central Washington |
| *Seattle Unit, Mountain Rescue Council | Seattle, Washington | Cascade Range Olympic Range |
| *Skagit Mountain Rescue | Mount Vernon, Washington | North Cascades |
| *Tacoma Unit, Mountain Rescue Council | Tacoma, Washington | Southern Washington Cascades and Mt. Rainier |
| *U. S. Navy Ground Search and Rescue | Sand Point Naval Air Station Seattle, Washington | Cascade Range |

WYOMING

| | | |
|---|---|---|
| Grand Teton National Park Service | National Park Headquarters Moose, Wyoming | Teton Range (during summer climbing season) |
| *Laramie Unit, Mountain Rescue | Laramie, Wyoming | Medicine Bow Mountains and Black Hills |

**Note:** Coordinating group for North America — Mountain Rescue Association, P. O. Box 67, Seattle 11, Washington 98111.


## Mountain Rescue Groups in English-Speaking Nations Outside of North America

NEW ZEALAND

The Federated Mountain Clubs of New Zealand

> A. P. Thomson,
> President
> P.O. Box 1604
> Wellington, New
> Zealand

12

GREAT BRITAIN

Due to limitations of space, it is not possible to list all of the many rescue organizations that are active in Great Britain. Rather than list only a few, and thereby ignore the many others that also deserve mention, the reader is referred for a complete listing to the book, *Mountain Rescue—Cave Rescue*, issued by The Mountain Rescue Committee, Chairman R. S. Piggot, located at Hill House, Cheadle Hulme, Stockport, Cheshire, England.

| *Group* | *Location* | *Area Covered* |
|---|---|---|
| INDIA | | |
| Mountain Rescue Section, Himalayan Mountaineering Institute | Darjeeling, India Tensing Norkay Delhi, India | |
| AFRICA | | |
| Mountain Club of Kenya | Robert Chambers, P. O. Box 5741, Nairobi | Kenya |
| Mountain Club of Uganda | | Uganda |
| Kilimanjaro Mountain Club | | Tanganyika |
| Outward Bound Mountain School | Loitokitok, Kenya | Kenya |
| Mountain Royal National Parks | Nyeri, Kenya | Kenya |
| Police Training School | Moshi, Tanganyika | Tanganyika |

# PREFACE

The first edition of this manual was designed to assist in the training of alpine rescuers. We have been pleased to see the equipment and techniques then described adopted not only throughout the Alps but in virtually every other world center of mountaineering.

Recent years have tremendously enriched and advanced our knowledge of mountain rescue. With the cooperation of rescuers in Austria and other countries, we have, during extensive field use, found and corrected faults of the methods set forth in 1948. Specialized devices have been simplified and their safety margin increased; innovations have been added to cope with more situations and terrains. However, the methods are fundamentally the same; they have been revised in the years since 1948, but not replaced.

In 1948 the Oesterreichischer Alpenverein invited experts from many countries to an International Rescue Congress. All who attended shared a deep concern for the future of mountaineering. From that concern was derived the notion of an organization devoted to the study and testing of rescue methods with the intent of gaining uniform standards applicable to the entire mountain world. That intent has since been realized by the formation of IKAR, the International Committee for Alpine Rescue, which officially endorses the equipment and techniques presented here.

Sheer muscle power is not enough for a demanding tour of difficult cliffs; neither is it enough for a rescue from those cliffs. Before a person can be a rescuer, he must first be a climber, completely familiar with mountaineering techniques and equipment. This manual assumes a complete competence on the part of the reader in the use of climbing equipment and techniques. Rescue work requires all the ordinary tools and techniques of mountaineering as well as the specialized equipment and methods described in the following pages.

In conclusion, let me express my deep personal hope that this manual will help to save lives and relieve distress wherever mountaineers travel, wherever they encounter misfortune.

**Wastl Mariner**


This English edition has been recognized as the official manual of the International Commission for Alpine Rescue.

Pontresina, November 30th, 1963

**Dr. med. Rudolf Campell**

# CONTENTS

# PART ONE

# SUMMER
# RESCUE

# SPECIALIZED RESCUE GEAR

The specialized rescue gear evolved in recent years has proven itself capable of coping with every rescue situation, whatever the nature of the terrain or the extent of the casualty's injuries. Moreover, the gear is so versatile that often a rescue requires only a single item of specialized equipment.

The **cable gear** for hoisting and lowering on cliffs and for belaying on steep slopes has immense advantages over older rescue methods using climbing rope.

The **mountain stretcher** is the most important single item of rescue equipment, making possible safe transport of any casualty over any terrain, whatever the injuries, whatever the difficulties.

The **carrying seat** and **carrying sack** are particuarly useful to small rescue parties, though they can only be employed when the condition of the casualty and the terrain allow.

The **rescuer's belt** is used both for hoisting and lowering slightly injured casualties and to attach them to other transport devices.

These five specialized devices, supplemented by the customary kit of an experienced mountaineer, compose the summer outfit of a mountain rescue group. The first requisite of potential rescuers, and the first function of rescue training, is complete competence in the use of this equipment.

## Cable Gear

The cable gear (Fig. 1) is used on any sort of precipitous terrain to hoist and lower casualties and to transport them by aerial tramway. The cable winch allows a casualty to be hoisted very great distances to a point of safety, frequently a much easier and faster means of evacuation than lowering. The components of the cable gear are described in the following paragraphs.

*Translator's note: Weights and measures in this translation are given in approximate English units, followed in parentheses by the exact metric units specified by Wastl Mariner.*

Of the **four steel cables** (Fig. 1-a), two are 325 feet (100 m) long and 1/5 inch (5 mm) in diameter, one is 165 feet (50 m) long and 1/5 inch (5 mm) in diameter, and one is 820 feet (250 m) long and 1/10 inch (2.5 mm) in diameter. The 1/5-inch (5 mm) cables have a breaking strength of about 4000 pounds (1900 kg); the 1/10-inch (2.5 mm) cable, about 1300 pounds (600 kg). The cables are made of galvanized steel strands wound around a hemp core. The ends are spliced and soldered into eyes.

The **brake drum** (Fig. 1-b) consists of a hardwood cylinder mounted in a U-shaped steel shackle fitted with a bolted screw connection for attaching a cable. On each side of the shackle are three buttonhead belaying pins for securing the cable during interruptions in lowering operations. The hardwood cylinder has a spiral-shaped groove to guide the cable; to prevent the cable from cutting into the wood, and also to reduce friction, the cylinder surface is covered with imbedded plastic pins.

**Four reels** (Fig. 1-c) made of thin sheet metal, pressed and welded, are used for cable storage and transport.

The **four coupling pieces** (Fig. 1-d) are used in pairs, two side pieces forming a round body when screwed together. The screws may easily be loosened simultaneously with a coin, hook, or knifeblade. When loosened they release one of the side pieces, thus making it possible to insert the two guy thimbles. The screws are secured by steel boxes pressed in place.

21

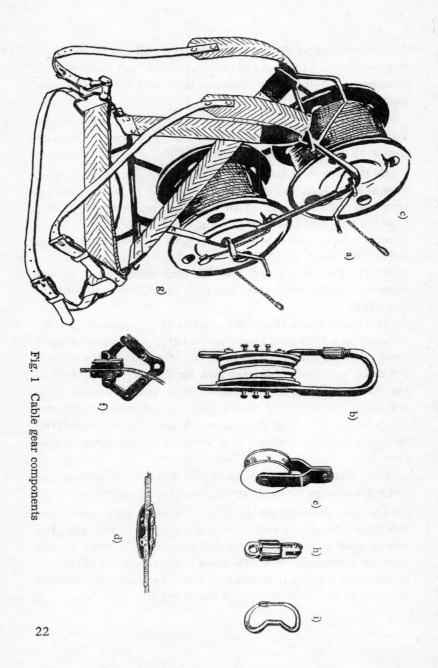

Fig. 1 Cable gear components

The **two pulleys** (Fig. 1-e) made of light metal have deep recesses which allow the coupling, as well as the cable, to pass through easily. Each pulley is suspended from two flat steel flanges which may be slipped by each other to allow the cable to be inserted quickly.

The **dog** (Fig. 1-f), which is used to secure the cable in a static position, consists of a ground plate with laterally opening friction jaws and rotating cam levers. The friction jaws, shaped to fit the cable, are pressed against the cable, when the dog is under load, by action of the levers.

A **carrying frame** with two cranks attached (Fig. 1-g), is used to transport the two cables and reels.

The **swivel** (Fig. 1-h) consists of a ball bearing or thrust bearing housed in a strong casing. The two eyes connected to the casing pivot on the bearing independently of each other. The rescuer and the cable can be separately attached to the casing, one to each eye. The casing components are secured by pins to prevent them from loosening. The swivel is used in lowering casualties down overhangs, and also in place of a safety carabiner to connect the casualty and rescuer to the cable, largely eliminating the disagreeable and sometimes dangerous spinning of persons being lowered through free space.

The **four safety carabiners** (Fig. 1-i) are used to connect the casualty and the rescuer to the cable and also to connect the cable to the anchor. They are constructed so that a ring screw prevents accidental opening of the snap.

The **cable winch** (Fig. 2) consists of the **lifting jack** and the **guide roller**.

The components of the **lifting jack** (Fig. 2-A) are a flat steel frame, a cable drum driven by hand-operated cranks and aluminum doublecone gears, and adjustable legs easily detached for transport. The cable drum, which is used for mounting or changing the cable by means of a knockout

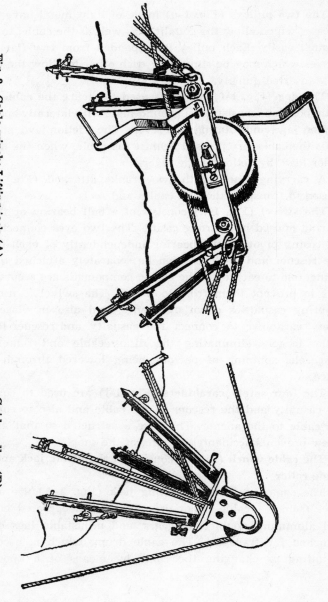

Fig. 2  Cable winch: Lifting jack (A)    Guide roller (B)

24

spindle, can also be removed easily from the frame. A safety device automatically locks the drum in case of any interruption during use.

The **guide roller** (Fig. 2-B) allows the cable to be guided under load in such a manner that it runs in the direction of the lifting jack frame, thus eliminating undesirable lateral stresses and making it easier for both the rescuer and the casualty to stay clear of the wall. The legs of the guide roller are adjustable and can be detached easily for transport.

**Maintenance**

After use, the steel cables should be completely dried and then either laid out straight or loosely coiled or looped on reels for storage. After each use, and before storage, each cable should be closely examined for damage. If every wire of any one strand is severed, the cable must be discarded, but a few broken wires do not reduce strength seriously. The cables should be wiped down periodically with a greased rag.

The brake drum must be treated regularly with some water-repellant compound such as linseed oil. If deep ruts appear in parts of a drum, it should be turned 180 degrees; if the ruts extend all the way around, it must be discarded.

All threaded and sliding parts of the cable gear should always be well lubricated.

# Mountain Stretcher

The mountain stretcher (Figs. 3—5) is used to transport any casualty, whatever his injuries, over any sort of terrain, either by lowering down cliffs, dragging on steep slopes, wheeling along trails, sliding over glaciers or snowfields, or carrying in the manner of ordinary stretchers.

The stretcher is constructed of thin-walled steel tubes. A pair of lower longerons bent upwards (Fig. 4-a) and a pair of upper longerons with a slightly less acute curve (Fig. 4-b) are rigidly connected at the ends by hinged button links (Fig.

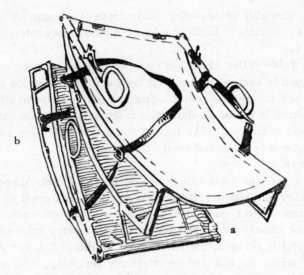

Fig. 3  Mountain stretcher, demounted for transport

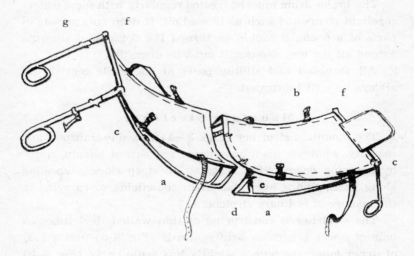

Fig. 4  Moutain stretcher, in position for assembly

4-c) converging at an acute angle, and connected in the middle by telescoping struts (Fig. 4-d) which facilitate rapid assembly and disassembly. Cotter pins on both sides (Fig. 4-e) prevent the two halves of the stretcher from coming apart during use. The pairs of longerons are connected laterally by cross struts (Fig. 4-f). At each end of the stretcher, two handles (Fig. 4-g) are attached in such a way that they can be rotated to any of four different positions at each of four different angles. The handles can be adjusted independently of each other for easy handling. A curved aluminum sheet (Fig. 3-a) is fitted between the upper steel tubes for the casualty's comfort and protection. On the lower longerons, two pairs of welded rings allow installation of either one or two balloon-tire bicycle wheels.

The single wheel (Fig. 5-b) may be fitted in any of three positions. A wheel either with or without a brake drum may be used. The braking device on the carrier itself (Fig. 5-a) is easily attached and removed. Two V-shaped pairs of struts (Fig. 5-b), hooked into the welded rings on the frame, support the wheel.

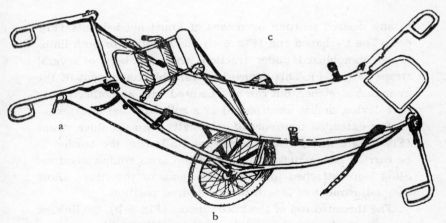

Fig. 5  Mountain stretcher with single wheel, assembled

Specially constructed forks are used to fasten twin wheels to the longerons, in any of several positions.

The adjustable device used both for traction and for knee support (Fig. 6) locks into any of several stops provided on the frame (Fig. 5-c). The device consists of two pairs of jointed metal rods connected at the joint by a rubber-covered knee support (Fig. 6-a). Threaded rods (Fig. 6-b) can be adjusted

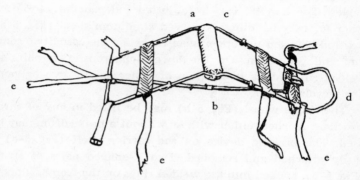

Fig. 6  Knee support and traction device

to any desired position by means of knurl-headed nuts (Fig. 6-c). The U-shaped end (Fig. 6-d) allows either or both limbs to be immobilized under traction, with the help of several straps (Fig. 6-e). This device is a valuable component of the mountain stretcher, but can also be used with any other transport device, and is unsurpassed as a splint for leg injuries.

For extended transport of a casualty, two shoulder straps (Fig. 7) are indispensable accessories, allowing the burden to be carried like a rucksack, leaving the arms completely free. Sling loops attached to rings at the ends of the straps allow easy adjustment of length to any desired position.

The threaded rod of the knee support (Fig. 6-b), the linkage between the two sections of the stretcher (Fig. 4-d), the cotter

28

pins (Fig. 4-e), and the handle joints (Fig. 4-c) should all be oiled occasionally. In winter use, the stretcher must be protected from rust.

Fig. 7   Shoulder straps for stretcher carriers

## Carrying Seat

The carrying seat (Fig. 8) is used to carry casualties whose injuries are such they can be transported safely in a sitting position. It can be employed in every sort of terrain where the attending rescuer can either walk or be lowered by a rope.

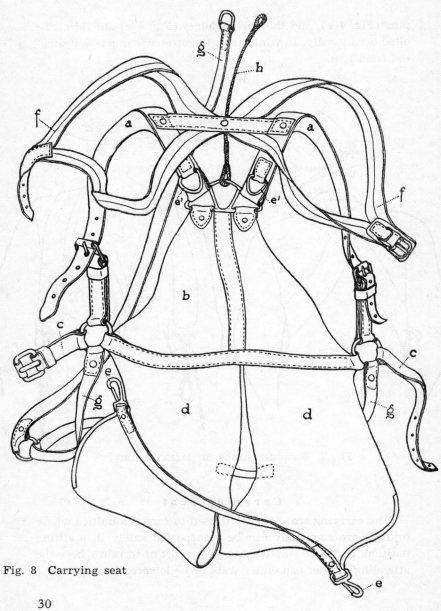

Fig. 8  Carrying seat

30

The seat, similar to a rucksack, consists of two carrying straps (Fig. 8-a) fastened to the triangular rear part (Fig. 8-b). The front strap (Fig. 8-c) is used to fasten the carrying seat to the rescuer. Two strips of downward-hanging canvas (Fig. 8-d) provide a seat for the casualty. The two strips, which are connected by two cross-belts fastened to the triangular rear part, support the thighs and buttocks of the casualty. To attach the casualty securely to the rear part and to prevent him from losing his balance, carabiners (Fig. 8-c) are snapped into the rings (Fig. 8-e). The shoulder straps (Fig. 8-f) are fitted to a cross piece between the carrying straps. When the seat is to be used for lowering a casualty, the rescuer ties himself to the end of the rope attached to the seat. bringing it forward from the rear between his legs and snapping it into the short steel cable (Fig. 8-h), thereby relieving himself of the weight of the casualty.

Leather parts of the carrying seat should be greased regutarly, as should all metal parts as a protection against rust. Any damaged seams must be repaired before further use. Storage should always be in a dry, well-ventilated location.


### Carrying Sack

The carrying sack (Fig. 9) is used to lower severely injured casualties down cliffs, to transport them by aerial tramway, and to carry them over moderate terrain. However, it must never be used when injuries are so severe as to require transport by rigid stretcher.

The carrying sack consists of a bottom part (Fig. 9-a) made of strong canvas and of two overlapping strips (Fig. 9-b) sewn longitudinally onto the upper side. The head is cut in the shape of a hood large enough to allow padding. The foot is shaped like a sack. The carrying sack is closed and secured by a cord running through grommets and hooks. Four strong cross-belts

(Fig. 9-c) with laterally protruding loops are sewn to the underside of the bottom part.

After each use, the carrying sack should be examined for damage, repaired if necessary, and stored in a dry, well-ventilated location.

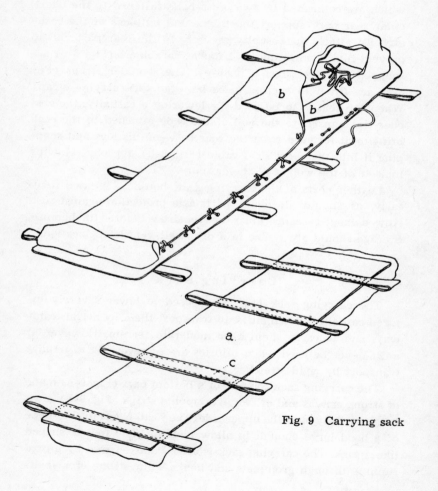

Fig. 9  Carrying sack

## Rescuer's Belt

The rescuer's belt (Fig. 10) is used to lower either a rescuer or a casualty with slight injuries. It may also sometimes be used to strap casualties to various other transport devices.

The belt consists of a strong strap approximately 12 feet (3,6 m) long and 2½ inches (60 mm) wide, with a clamp-type buckle attached at one end and a triangular ring in the middle.

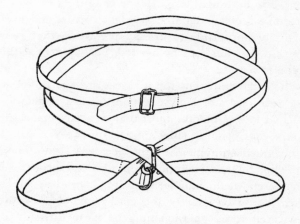

Fig. 10   Rescuer's belt

# 2

# TRANSPORT WITH SPEZIALIZED GEAR

Ideally, a rescue group should always set forth on a mission carrying every item of gear required by the accident situation, but nothing more. However, rarely does a rescue group receive a clear, detailed accident report, and even then it is virtually impossible to predict precisely what rescue kit and first aid supplies will be needed, particularly if the accident scene is remote.

Selection of equipment for a rescue mission involves such difficult decisions and heavy responsibilities it should never be entrusted to any but the most experienced personnel available. Only one general rule applies in every case: there is never too much equipment at the accident scene, and rarely enough. Though it is essential to minimize rescuers' loads to keep the rescue team mobile, gear left behind as superfluous may turn out to be exactly the gear demanded by the situation; without it the mission may be more difficult, or may fail. The first condition of a successful rescue is that the team be outfitted with the proper equipment selected by rescue leaders who have the judgment and foresight that comes only with long experience.

## Rescue from Cliffs

### Approaching the Accident Scene

An accident scene located in the lower 650 feet (200 m) of a cliff usually can be best approached from below (Fig. 11), the rescuers ascending in one or more rope teams. When the transport method can be decided beforehand, rescuers often

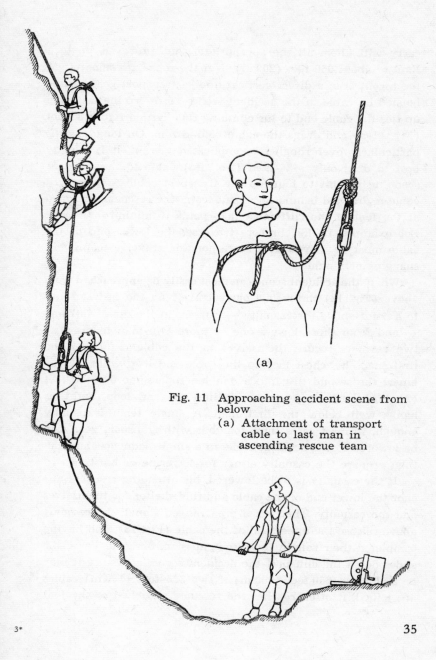

(a)

Fig. 11  Approaching accident scene from below

(a) Attachment of transport cable to last man in ascending rescue team

carry with them all the appropriate gear. However, up to a limit of about 650 feet (200 m) — if the rocks are smooth and the ascent is in a direct vertical line — transport gear can be hoisted by cable to the accident scene. To do so, the last man up ties the cable end to his climbing rope with a figure 8 knot (Fig. 11-a) and drags the cable behind him. On long ascents, particularly over rough or complicated terrain, it is usually best to drag only a ⅛-inch (2.5 mm) cable to the accident scene, using this to haul up the transport cable. Whenever a cable is dragged behind an ascent team, the rescuers stationed at the foot of the cliff must take pains to minimize friction. For example, if the climbers traverse, the lower end of the cable must be moved in a corresponding traverse to prevent snagging or jamming.

When the accident scene can most easily be **approached from above** (Fig. 12) the rescue party travels by the fastest route to a point above the casualty — but *not* in the direct fall line — and from there lowers one or more two-man teams. The two rescuers secure themselves to the cable as follows: the first snaps his chest loop to the cable-end loop with a carabiner; the second ties into a doubled rope some 6 to 10 feet (2—3 m) long, snaps this rope into the end loop, and thus hangs well below the first man. A single team is usually enough. In most cases they, together with transport gear, can be lowered to the accident scene in a single sequence, and can then prepare the casualty either for lowering or hoisting.

If the casualty is to be lowered, his attending rescuers anchor the lower end of the cable and find shelter for themselves and the casualty. Then, on a prearranged signal, the rescuers above release the upper end of the cable (Fig. 13), and having completed their role in the rescue mission, descend. The cable slides down the cliff past the accident scene, and since it may be as long as 650 feet (200 m) if two 325-foot (100 m) cables are joined, it often reaches the rescuers stationed at the foot

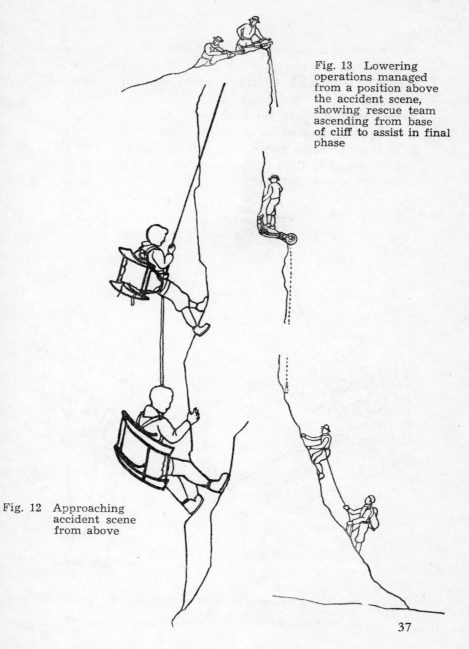

Fig. 13 Lowering
operations managed
from a position above
the accident scene,
showing rescue team
ascending from base
of cliff to assist in final
phase

Fig. 12 Approaching
accident scene
from above

37

of the wall. If it does not, they must climb up to the dangling cable end before transport can begin. This freedrop method cannot be used unless the cliff is quite steep and entirely free from rockfall.

**Preparing the Casualty for Transport**

A slightly injured or exhausted person partially able to help himself can be moved safely in the **rescuer's belt** (Fig. 14). To keep him from falling backward, he is secured to the cable with a chest harness.

Fig. 14   Left: Casualty being lowered in rescuer's belt, with chest harness attached

Right: Casualty in rescuer's belt, ready for lowering

Fig. 15  Casualty being lowered in carrying seat, aided by attending rescuer

If the casualty can be moved in a sitting position, and is in no danger of fainting, the easiest means of transport is the **carrying seat** (Fig. 15), to which he is secured in the same way as with the auxiliary seat. On steep cliffs, since the casualty is supported entirely by the cable, the only effort required of the rescuer is to provide protection from wall collisions.

By proper adjustment of lines, the **carrying sack** (Fig. 16) can be used to move the casualty in either a horizontal or crouching position. The crouching position is best unless there

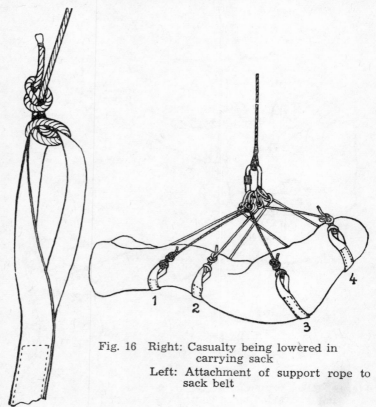

Fig. 16   Right: Casualty being lowered in carrying sack

Left: Attachment of support rope to sack belt

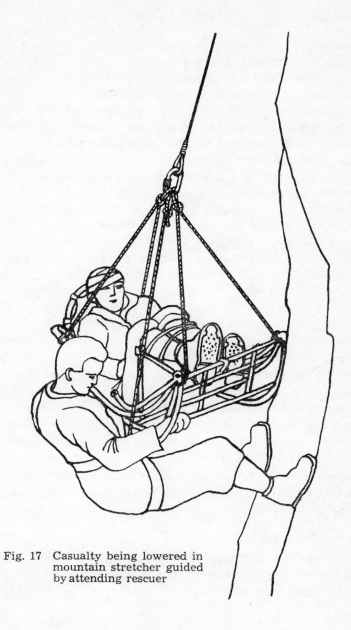

Fig. 17  Casualty being lowered in
         mountain stretcher guided
         by attending rescuer

are spinal injuries or unusual complications. The carrying belts are rigged so that belts 1 and 3 are connected by one line on each side, belts 2 and 4 by another. The four lines, two on each side, are secured to a safety carabiner attached to the cable.

The **mountain stretcher** (Fig. 17) is not only easy to use but provides maximum protection and comfort to the casualty, who can be splinted directly to the stretcher in various ways, depending on his injuries. A major advantage of the stretcher is that once a casualty is tied in, he need not be resplinted until he reaches the hospital.

The stretcher is rigged with two lines to the front bar and two lines to the rear bar. (For clarity, the illustration shows only a single line to each bar.) These lines are tied with figure 8 knots into a safety carabiner attached to the cable. To protect the casualty from direct contact with the rock, the lines next to the cliff should be shorter than the outside lines. When the stretcher is used for a sustained period, it should be secured to the transport cable by steel cables rather then ropes.

The attending rescuer travels in a rescuer's seat attached by ropes to the safety carabiner. The lines should be carefully adjusted to ensure that the stretcher rides at the level of the rescuer's chest. In this and in every other transport situation, the rescuer and casualty should wear helmets or "hard hats" as protection against rockfall. *(Translator's note: Helmets are not shown in any of the illustrations in this manual, but are essential equipment on rescues.)*

Before transport begins, all rescuers must agree on a set of signals by voice, loudspeakers, radio, or telephone to cover any communication need.

### Lowering the Casualty

To prepare for lowering, the rescue party first anchors the brake drum to several securely placed, interconnected pitons (Fig. 18) or to some solid feature of the terrain (Fig. 19). The

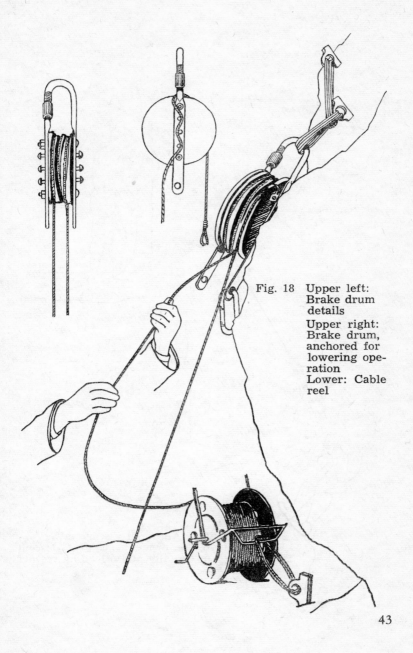

Fig. 18 Upper left:
Brake drum
details
Upper right:
Brake drum,
anchored for
lowering ope-
ration
Lower: Cable
reel

43

Fig. 19    Anchored rescuer using brake drum to control descent of casualty and attending rescuer

44

anchor must be arranged so that the load presses the brake drum against the rock, thus preventing it from jumping when under stress and causing a jerky cable run.

The second step is to wind the cable around the sheaves of the brake drum (Fig. 18): a single turn if the weight of the casualty and the angle of the cliff are both moderate, two turns for a heavier casualty or a steeper cliff. The loaded leg of the cable must be placed next to the wall; otherwise it may bind the slack leg against the rock. The slack cable emerging from the top of the drum is strung through the belay pins on the drum shackle and remains there while the rescuers prepare the casualty for transport.

When both the casualty and his attending rescuer are secured to a safety carabiner attached to the cable, the brake drum operator removes the cable from the shackle pins and lets it slide smoothly and evenly over the drum (Fig. 19). The operator needs sufficient slack to ensure a smooth cable run; if a cable spool (Fig. 18) is not at hand, he must — before lowering begins — coil the cable in large neat loops near the anchor. If the brake drum begins to jump during lowering, the operator greases the sheaves with sunburn cream or any similar lubricating substance available.

The attending rescuer avoids wall collisions by leaning out with his feet planted firmly against the rock (Fig. 19) and by adjusting his movements to the lowering pace. If the pace is too fast or too slow, he requests a change by prearranged signals.

If the casualty and his attending rescuer have not reached safe terrain within one cable length, lowering ceases while a second cable is attached (Fig. 20). First, the loaded cable is secured on the shackle pins (Fig. 20-A). Next, the eyelets of the second cable and of the already loaded cable are connected by a coupling piece (Fig. 20-B), taking care to tighten the coupling screw evenly and firmly. The loaded cable is now freed

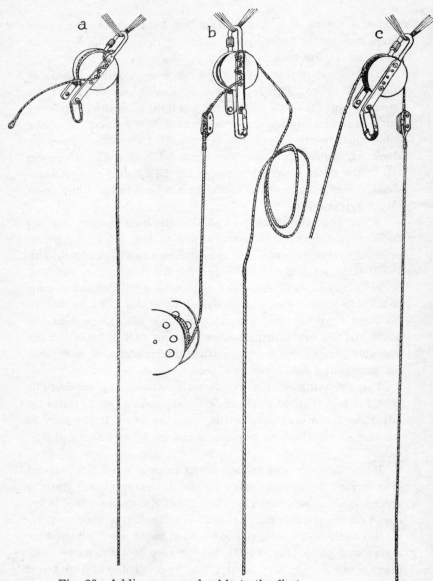

Fig. 20   Adding a second cable to the first
to allow continued lowering

from the shackle pins and lowering resumes, the coupling piece running easily over the spiral-shaped drum sheave (Fig. 20-C). When the cliff is sufficiently steep and smooth, a casualty can be lowered as much as three cable lengths — 1000 feet (300 m) — in a continuous sequence from a single belay position; under exceptionally favorable circumstances, even farther.

When the cliff is taller than 1000 feet (300 m), usually a second belay position must be installed, rigged identically to the first (Fig. 21). If the need is foreseen at the start of rescue operations, a team ascends and prepares a rockfall-sheltered belay station in the fall line from the upper belay. The site need not be in the exact fall line if the cliff is smooth and the casualty hangs a considerable distance below the upper belay; under such conditions the attending rescuer can easily pendulum a horizontal distance of 30 to 45 feet (10—15 m). When the casualty reaches the lower belay station, a waiting rescuer snaps the new cable to the safety carabiner from which the casualty is suspended (Fig. 21). When the load has been shifted to the new cable, the upper cable is released and lowering continues from the new belay.

If there is any danger of dislodging rocks, the upper rescue groups must remain at their stations until the casualty has been evacuated from the cliff. Rescuers may then descend in one of two ways:

1. The rescuers on the cliff haul up the cables or, if conditions allow, drop them to the base of the cliff. They then ascend to the top of the cliff and descend by an easier route.

2. On any very long and difficult cliff, the cable gear provides the fastest and easiest way to evacuate rescuers. First, the upper rescue team replaces its brake drum with a pulley and the lower rescue team re-anchors its brake drum in a position suitable for controlling the cable on an upward run to the pulley (Fig. 22). The upper team then descends on the cable, belayed by the lower team. Upon reaching the lower station,

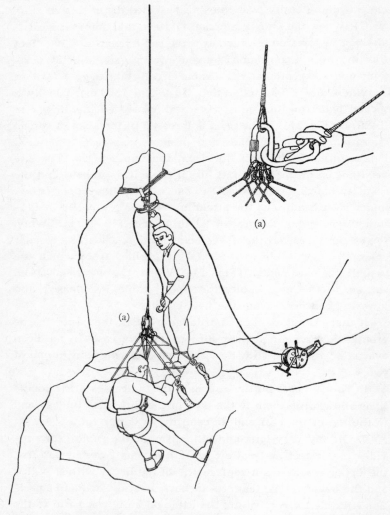

(a)

(a)

Fig. 21  Transferring the load from an upper lowering station to
a second station

the rescuers pull the cable down from above, abandoning the pulley. Further lowering continues in the same way, belayed through a brake drum anchored and operated by the rescue team at the foot of the cliff.

If the accident scene is less than 650 feet (200 m) above the base of the cliff, and if access to the scene is easier from below, then the approach should be made from below. In that case, the rescuers anchor a pulley at the accident scene, as described above (Fig. 22), and secure the casualty to the cable. The rescuers at the foot of the cliff then belay the lowering through an anchored brake drum. Control from below requires twice as much cable, but this is usually a minor disadvantage, since the extra cable can be carried to the foot of the cliff with relatively little effort. There are several major advantages. First, the brake drum can be anchored more easily at the base of a cliff than higher up, on a ledge. Second, a position can usually be selected which allows constant observation of the descending casualty and his attending rescuer. Third, the rescue team on the wall can be quickly evacuated.

## Hoisting the Casualty

When the accident scene lies high on a cliff and there is a relatively easy approach to a point directly above, the preferred evacuation direction is upward, hoisting the casualty with a cable winch, rather than lowering him a long distance down difficult cliffs. *(Translator's note: Other winches, including a Yugoslavian manually operated model and a Swiss design utilizing a pump lever, are currently being tested by the IKAR.)* Anchoring and operating a cable winch requires a flat surface at least 6 feet by 3 feet (2 x 1 m), but since a hoisting station is most commonly placed on a summit ridge, sufficient space is usually available. Hoisting can also be performed with a winch from a station below the casualty, similarly to use of a brake drum for lowering.

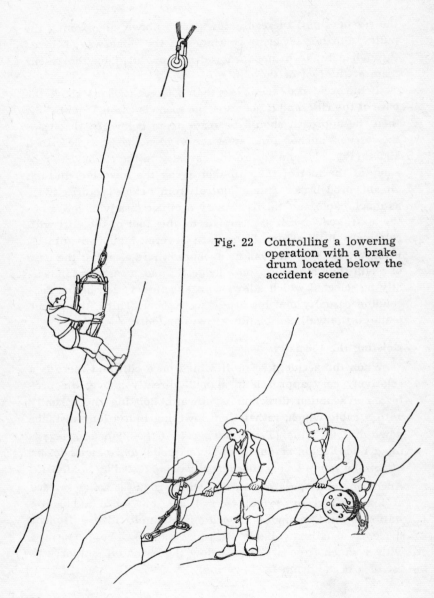

Fig. 22   Controlling a lowering
operation with a brake
drum located below the
accident scene

First, the winch and guide roller are anchored, either horizontally (standing) or vertically (hanging). Care must be taken that both winch and roller are rigged so that they will not be tilted by the load. To minimize lateral play and ensure smooth cable runout from the spool, both winch and guide roller should lie in the same plane.

Next, the winch drum is removed from its frame and wound carefully with five to eight side-by-side turns of cable. After the drum has been replaced in its frame, the cable must be checked to make sure the loaded leg enters the bottom of the winch. If possible, the cable should enter and leave the winch in the same plane.

A ratchet automatically locks the winch under load, preventing the cable from running out. As an added precaution, the lock pin on the winch frame should be inserted into the drum whenever the operator is not directly controlling the winch.

Finally, the cable is threaded over the guide roller.

The first step in evacuation by hoisting is to lower a rescuer to the accident scene to prepare the casualty for transport. Both the casualty and the attending rescuer can easily be hoisted by two rescuers operating the winch cranks, a third rescuer keeping the incoming cable under slight tension as he coils it on a spool anchored nearby. Two winches and two cables should be used for any hoist over a great vertical distance or over a cliff very much broken by ridges, gullies, and slabs. Great care must be taken at all times in handling the cable to avoid dislodging rockfall onto those suspended from the cable.

Generally, a long hoist is only possible with a cable winch. If a winch is not available, a block-and-tackle can be rigged with cable gear (Figs. 23 and 24). Although a block-and-tackle is not as efficient as a winch, under good conditions it allows a casualty to be hoisted by two rescuers, one hauling while the

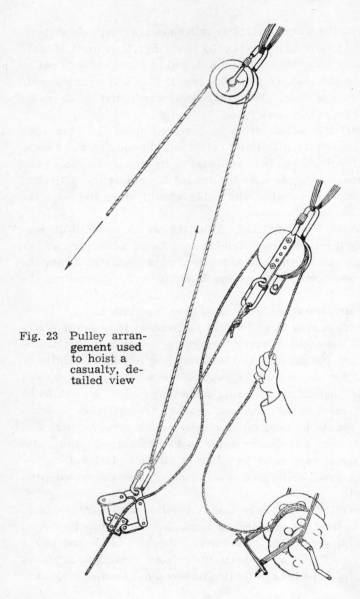

Fig. 23 Pulley arrangement used to hoist a casualty, detailed view

52

other manages the cable. With sufficient manpower at the scene, a casualty and attending rescuer can be hoisted together by block-and-tackle.

A simple variety of the block-and-tackle (Fig. 23) is rigged for hoisting in the following manner:

1. The cable leading to the casualty is threaded through an anchored brake drum and fixed to the belay pins on the shackle.

2. A rope is tied to the shackle eyelet of the brake drum either with a figure 8 knot or with a fisherman's knot and double loop.

3. The dog is clamped to the cable some 10 to 20 feet (3— 6 m) from the brake drum.

4. The rope tied to the brake drum is strung down through a carabiner snapped to the dog (Fig. 23-1), or preferably to a pulley (Fig. 24), and then up and over an anchored pulley (Fig. 23-2), and finally down to a rescuer.

The simple block-and-tackle illustrated in Figure 23 gives a theoretical mechanical advantage of 2, since the travel distance of the load up the cliff is half the travel distance of the pulley rope pulled down by the rescuer. The second rescuer hauls in cable slack until the dog hits the brake drum. The cable is then secured on the shackle pins while the dog is unclamped, moved down the cable, and reclamped to begin another sequence. To attain maximum travel in each sequence, thus minimizing hoisting time, the dog should be moved as far as possible from the brake drum.

Figure 24 illustrates the preferred method of rigging a block-and-tackle with cable gear if the terrain is suitable and proper equipment is available.

Fig. 24  Pulley arrangement used to hoist a casualty, over-all view

## Transport by Aerial Cableway

An aerial tramway (Fig. 25) can be used to transport casu-

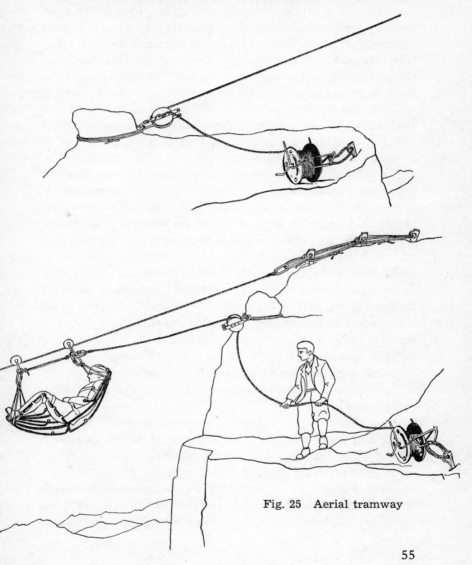

Fig. 25  Aerial tramway

alties down very rugged or rotten cliffs or across gorges. However, rigging a tramway is generally so complicated and time-consuming it is first choice only when several casualties must be evacuated, when the terrain presents exceptionally good opportunities for rigging, or when the terrain makes any other transport method extremely difficult or impossible. Maximum potential length of a tramway depends on the angle of the slope. A nearly horizontal tramway must not exceed a length of 1000 feet (300 m) without intermediate supports; if the angle is more than 45 degrees, the length may exceed 1500 feet (500 m), in which case two sets of steel cables are required.

When a rescue group at the foot of a cliff has decided to use a cableway, it should first determine the approximate route, length, and anchor points of the tramway. A rescue team then takes the easiest approach to the accident scene, but makes that approach by way of the preselected upper tramway station. Sometimes rescuers may carry enough $^1/_{10}$-inch (2.5 mm) cable to build the cableway. If not, they must in any event carry enough such cable to reach the bottom of the cliff. In the latter case, a rock weighing about 5 pounds (2—3 kg) is fastened to the end of the carried cable and is lowered down the steepest and smoothest portion of the cliff to its foot. The rescuers below attach the transport cable to the lowered cable, and the upper team then hoists the transport cable.

When a gorge must be bridged by aerial cableway, usually a team must descend to the bottom of the gorge to establish cable connections.

Once the transport cable has been extended between the upper and lower stations, both ends are anchored. The cable should *never* be wrapped around anchor rocks; instead, the cable eye should be snapped into carabiners attached to rope slings tied to the rocks. All sharp rock edges should first be rounded off with a piton hammer or padded with spare clothing or equipment. When the anchors have been rigged, rescuers at the upper base connect the cable to the anchor slings with a carabiner. Rescuers at the lower base then stretch the cable taut with a winch or a block-and-tackle, wind it onto a brake drum, and secure it to the shackle pins.

Casualties may be transported in a rescuer's belt, carrying sack, or mountain stretcher. Only one person should be on the tramway at a time. The casualty's carrying device is attached to the belaying cable similarly as in lowering, and is suspended from two runners used as trolleys on the transport cable (Fig. 25).

Speed of descent is controlled by the belaying cable, held by a brake drum operated by a single rescuer. A casualty can be allowed to move much more rapidly along a tramway than on a lowering cable, but the belaying cable must still be paid out evenly and smoothly to ensure a comfortable ride.

The aerial tramway has rarely been used for actual rescues. Despite theoretical advantages, a tramway usually takes far longer to rig than a belay for cable lowering, and therefore at present is practical only in exceptional cases. However, rigging may become much easier and faster if dependable rocket-propelled heaving lines are developed. The progress made in recent years allows us to hope for further improvements. Until now, the major use of the aerial tramway has been at rescue exercises in demonstrations designed to increase spectator attendance.

### Rescue from Steep Slopes

Transport down slopes not steep enough for lowering (less than 45 degrees, approximately) but not flat enough for carrying or wheeling, can be quite difficult. This portion of the alpine realm is often characterized by large boulders fallen from the cliffs above, or by rotten rock, or by steep grass and gravel offering no foothold. Reaching timberline does not eliminate all these problems; indeed, tough mats of alpine scrub may complicate the situation.

The best transport device in such terrain is the mountain stretcher (Fig. 26). If it has been in use for lowering down cliffs, the rope slings at the foot of the stretcher are unhooked from the safety carabiners and the stretcher is turned into the fall line. A rescuer ties himself to the lower end of the stretcher, facing uphill, and pulls the stretcher downhill on its runners. As before, the stretcher is belayed from above through a brake drum. Since the brake drum carries less load than on cliffs, the number of cable turns around the drum can be reduced.

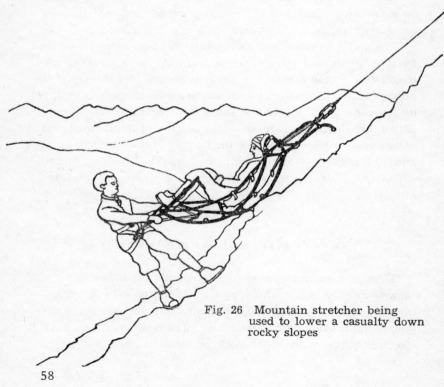

Fig. 26  Mountain stretcher being used to lower a casualty down rocky slopes

On steep snow, ice, and grass, the method is similar, though it is usually better for the attending rescuer to face downhill (Fig. 27).

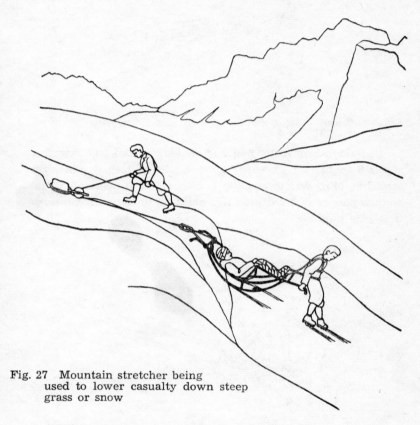

Fig. 27  Mountain stretcher being used to lower casualty down steep grass or snow

The brake drum can be secured by pitons, as on rock, but may also be anchored from a bollard cut into the slope (Fig. 28). To assure a smooth cable run, the drum should be thoroughly dampened with snow or ice; if the sheaves are partly damp and partly dry, the drum tends to jerk.

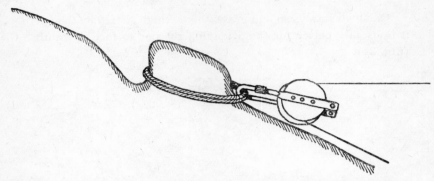

Fig. 28  Snow or ice bollard for anchoring a lowering operation

In terrain broken by many short ledges, two tree branches about 6 to 12 feet (2—4 m) long should be lashed under the stretcher (Fig. 29) to cushion bounces. For transport on glaciers, a pair of skis with the tips pointing to the rear can serve the same purpose.

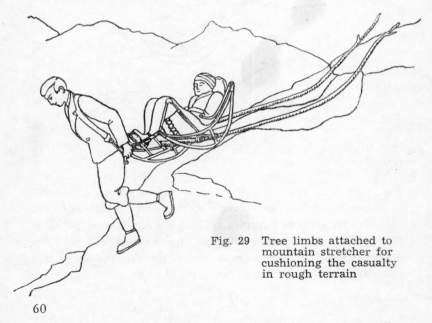

Fig. 29  Tree limbs attached to mountain stretcher for cushioning the casualty in rough terrain

By linking cables, a casualty can be lowered down a homogeneous slope of snow, grass, or scree as much as 1500 feet (500 m) while belayed from a single anchor. If less cable is available, lowering is done in relays (Fig. 30). When sufficient rescuers are on hand, the cable is divided between two teams, one belaying the casualty down to a lower anchor being prepared by the second team, and so on, leapfrog fashion. However, leapfrog lowering demands both favorable terrain and faultless coordination.

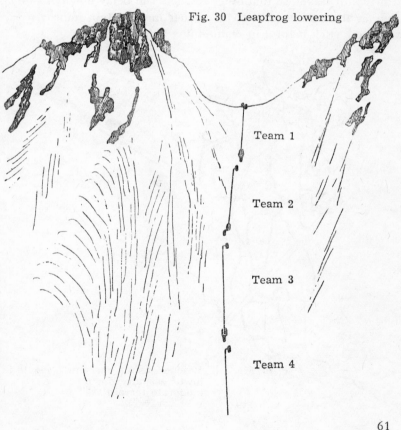

Fig. 30   Leapfrog lowering

Team 1

Team 2

Team 3

Team 4

61

## Rescue from Moderate Terrain

There are rescue dangers and difficulties on trails, meadows, scree, and low-angle rock slopes, but transport over such terrain is mainly a matter of much time and much energy — the more so if proper equipment is lacking or is used improperly.

When a casualty can be transported in a sitting position, the carrying seat is the best device (Fig. 31). The rescuer turns his anchor strap to his back for downhill travel, to his front for uphill travel, so that other rescuers can belay down or pull up, as the case requires. The rescuer may find an improvised walking stick helpful in maintaining balance.

Fig. 31 Rescuer using carrying seat to lower casualty down moderate terrain

The mountain stretcher should be used to transport a casualty with serious injuries (Figs. 32—37), particularly if he has been splinted to the stretcher during a previous phase of the rescue and transfer to another device might aggravate his injuries. The wheel, or wheels, are mounted in the center position of the stretcher, which can then be guided by two rescuers over the most primitive of trails. The shoulder straps provide traction to the rescuers when climbing, braking when des-

Fig. 32   Mountain stretcher, with
          single wheel attached to center,
          being used by two rescuers to
          transport casualty down trail

cending. Two wheels are obviously best for any broad path. A single wheel supports the stretcher on a single point, so that it may be maneuvered on even the most narrow and crooked of tracks. On very rocky terrain, on or off the trail, the man in the rear balances the stretcher by lifting the handlebars, thus protecting the casualty from jarring. Such care also minimizes strain on the stretcher, and should therefore be used even when transporting a corpse.

On well-maintained trails and smooth slopes, the stretcher can be rigged as a wheelbarrow, with the wheel mounted front

Fig. 33   Mountain stretcher, with single wheel attached to the rear, being used by one rescuer to transport casualty down trail

or rear. Since shocks are greatest near the wheel, it should be mounted at the casualty's foot when he has injuries to the head or upper body, and at his head when he has injuries to the legs or lower body. If necessary, a single rescuer can transport a casualty wheelbarrow-style, but generally two rescuers should be used. When a third rescuer is on hand, two men should walk behind the stretcher, one holding each handlebar. On rough trails such control is essential to balanced, cushioned transport. On steep terrain, ropes should be tied through the handlebar holes for braking and as a safety measure against runaways.

When it is necessary to transport a casualty a long distance uphill, a pulley anchored above can be very helpful. The cable should be rigged as far from ground level as possible to minimize friction and rockfall.

**Fig. 34** Mountain stretcher, with single wheel attached to the front, being used to transport casualty uphill

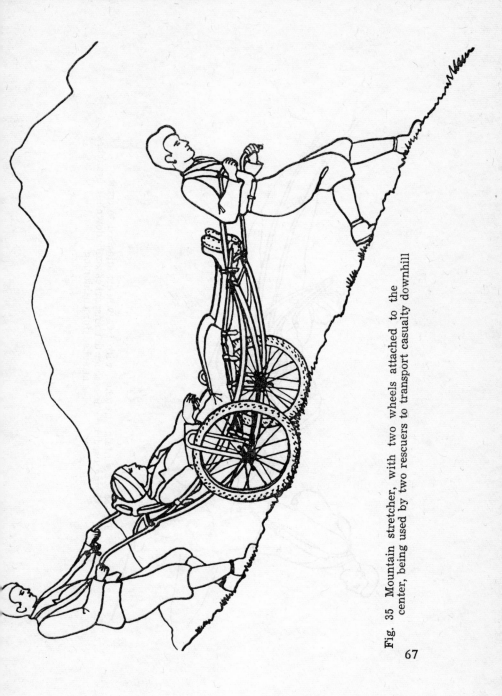

Fig. 35  Mountain stretcher, with two wheels attached to the center, being used by two rescuers to transport casualty downhill

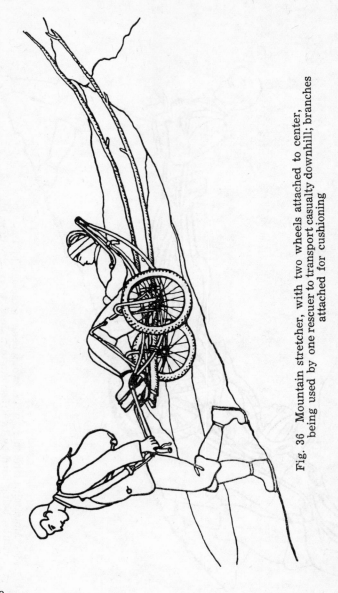

Fig. 36 Mountain stretcher, with two wheels attached to center, being used by one rescuer to transport casualty downhill; branches attached for cushioning

Fig. 37   Mountain stretcher being carried

# IMPROVISED RESCUE GEAR

Specialized rescue equipment is not always readily available at the accident scene, and in such cases it is necessary to transport casualties with nothing more than ordinary mountaineering equipment. Improvised transport demands the very highest degree of skill and experience, particularly over difficult terrain, and is always makeshift at best. However, methods based upon those developed for use with specialized equipment often can be adapted for use with rope, carabiners, slings, pitons, and any available natural materials, such as tree branches.

## Knots

Rope handling is basic to any and every mountain rescue. The following paragraphs describe the most important knots and their uses, together with their advantages and disadvantages.

The **bowline** (Fig. 38) is the most dependable and versatile of all knots. It can be tied quickly under any conditions and adjusted easily around the waist for a snug fit, uses a minimum amount of rope, and can be untied even when wet or after having tightened up under tension. For ascents where free falls are possible, a suspender-like **shoulder loop** (Fig. 39) can be rigged with a small length of rope. This sling holds the chest loop in the desired position and permits shifting of the knot around the body.

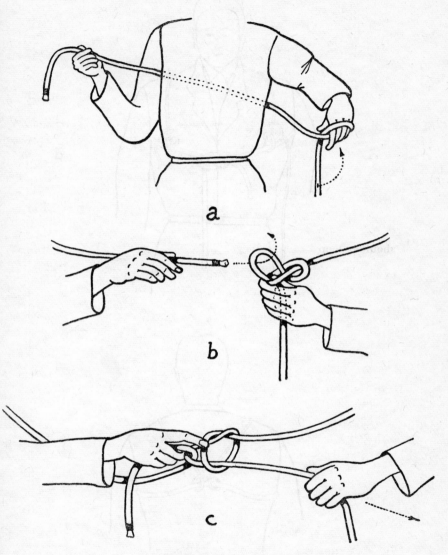

a

b

c

Fig. 38   Bowline knot, steps in tying

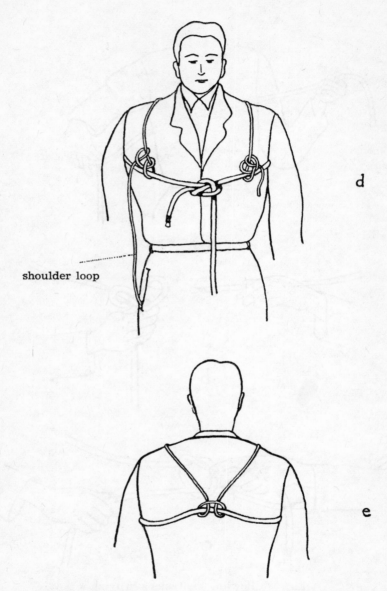

shoulder loop

d

e

Fig. 39  Bowline knot in position, with shoulder loop

The **chest harness** (Fig. 40-a) is especially good for rescues in moderately difficult terrain where it may be necessary to rope and unrope several times, for roping up on glaciers, and is also used on easier climbs which require only intermittent belays. A piece of rope 15 feet (4 m) long and ¼ inch (6-8 mm) in diameter is passed twice around the chest and secured with a bowline. The long end is thrown over the left shoulder, is pulled through the two strands across the back, passes over the right shoulder to the front like a suspender, and is tied to the short end of the rope with a square knot or a bowline. A safety carabiner is used to anchor the chest harness to the climbing rope.

The **rappel sling** (Fig. 40-b) is used as a rescue seat and as a rappel seat. As previously described, the sling is grasped in the middle, passed from behind the thighs to the front, where the two parts are snapped together into a safety carabiner. The rest of the rope makes a loop diagonally upward over the hips, across the back horizontally, and around to the front of the body, where it is adjusted for snugness and tied with a bowline.

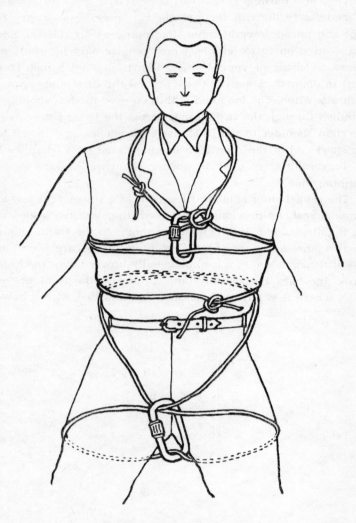

Fig. 40  Upper: Chest harness
Lower: Rappel sling

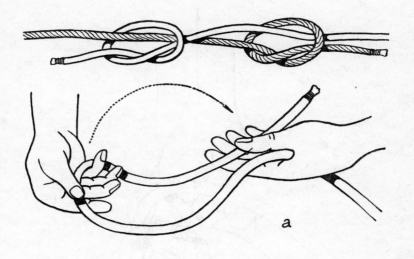

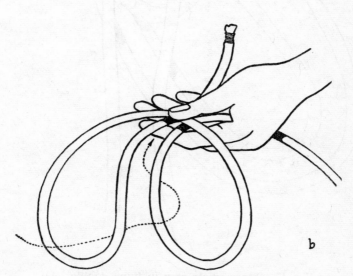

Fig. 41   Upper: Fisherman's knot
Lower: Initial steps in tying double loop

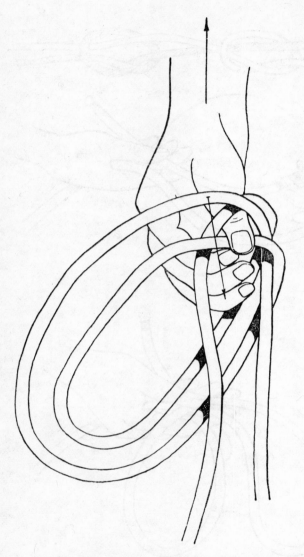

C'

Fig. 42    Intermediate step in tying double loop

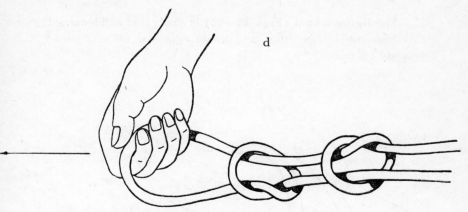

d

Fig 43   Final step in tying double loop

The **fisherman's knot with double loop** (Figs. 41—43) can be used to join ropes and also to rig various slings. It tightens automatically and is easily loosened.

The **square knot** (Fig. 44) should be used to join ropes only when the load is constant, since the knot loosens if rope tension slackens.

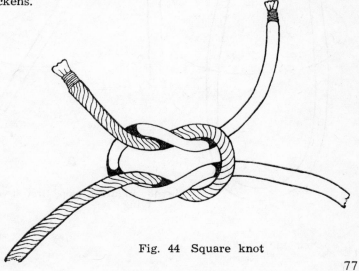

Fig. 44   Square knot

The **figure 8 knot** (Figs. 45—46) is easily tied and loosened; its best use is for slings and knots expected to hold under steady tension.

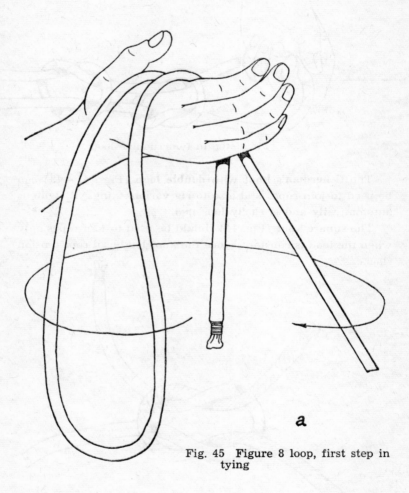

a

Fig. 45 **Figure 8 loop, first step in** tying

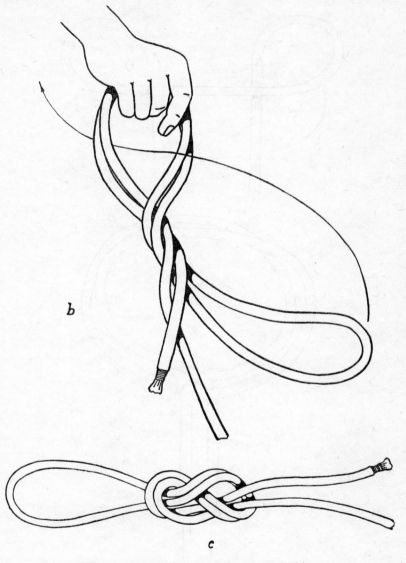

b

c

Fig. 46  Figure 8 loop, final steps in tying

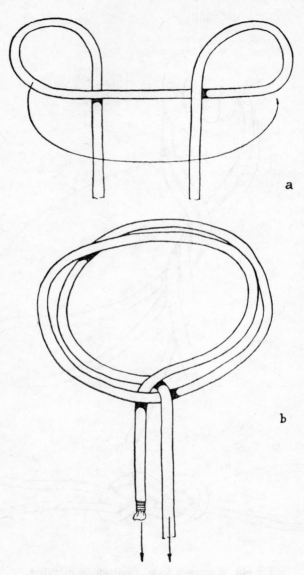

a

b

Fig. 47  Clove hitch, steps in tying

The **clove hitch** (Fig. 47) is used for connecting the climbing rope to the chest harness with a carabiner, for self-belaying slings, for rescue hitches of all sorts, and for secure attachment to any circular object.

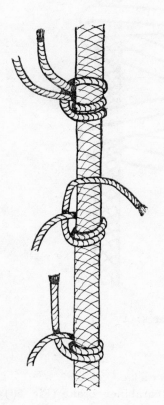

The **ring hitch** (Fig. 39-b) is one of the simplest, most-used knots for fastening ropes and slings to poles and other circular objects.

The **Prusik knot** (Fig. 48) grips tightly when loaded but slides freely when tension is relaxed. In tying the knot, the second winding must be placed inside the first. When the two ropes that are to be connected have nearly the same diameter or are covered with ice, the knot should be tied in a smaller connecting cord, as illustrated, as a guarantee against knot failure.

Fig. 48  Prusik knot

The **carabiner (Bachmann) knot** (Fig. 49) is superior to the Prusik when casualties are being hoisted with wet ropes, necessitating frequent shifts of the clamp knot.

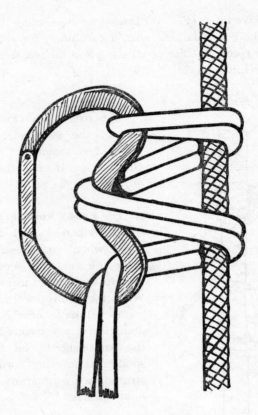

Fig. 49  Carabiner knot


### Carabiner Brake

For improvised lowerings, the carabiner brake (Fig. 50) and the climbing rope, taken together, substitute for the specialized cable gear. A single brake can be rigged with two carabiners, a double brake with four carabiners. Pitons, rock, cord, or ice ax shafts can be employed as carabiner substitutes.

82

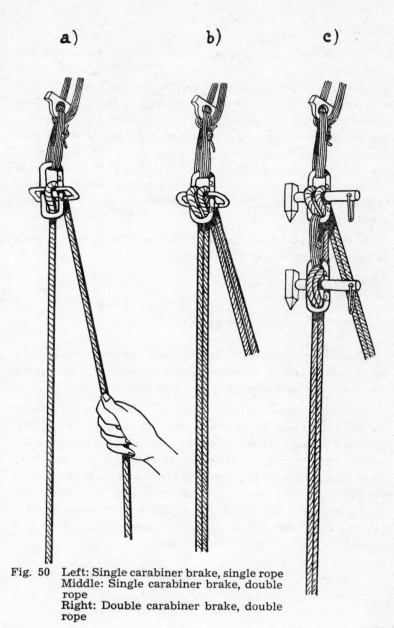

a)        b)        c)

Fig. 50    Left: Single carabiner brake, single rope
            Middle: Single carabiner brake, double
            rope
            Right: Double carabiner brake, double
            rope

A **single brake** is rigged as follows: Place a dependable anchor sling around a rock or through pitons. Snap a carabiner into the anchor sling, making sure the gate faces upward. Run a loop of rope through the carabiner, back to front, so that the loaded rope-end lies underneath the unloaded end. Place the second carabiner through the loop at right angles to the first carabiner, making sure the gate faces down. The rope *must* run over the solid part of the second, or braking, carabiner; if the gate of the braking carabiner is placed upward, the rope will force the gate open when it comes under load, causing a fall.

A **double brake** is rigged in the same manner by adding two more carabiners or substitutes.

### Rope Seats

The **single rescue seat** (Figs. 51—54) can be substituted for the rescuer's belt in lowering a rescuer or a slightly injured person. The rappel sling (Fig. 40) may also be used.

The single seat is rigged from an 8-foot (2.5 m) end of climbing rope and an 11½-foot (3.5 m) rope sling. The two loops are placed over the thighs to form a seat. To prevent the person from falling backward, a 12-foot (3.5 m) length of ¼-inch (7 mm) rope is grasped in the middle and attached to the climbing rope with a Prusik knot. The two ends of the sling are tied together with a figure 8 knot about 6 inches (15 cm) from the Prusik knot. The remaining part is tied around the chest as in the chest harness.

Fig. 51   Rigging a single rescue seat, steps 1 and 2

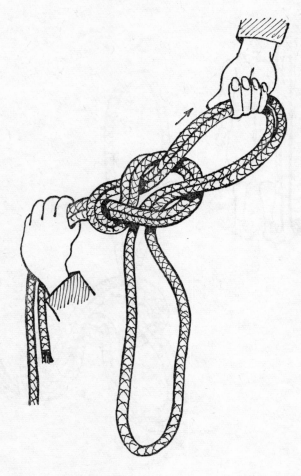

Fig. 52   Single rescue seat, step 3

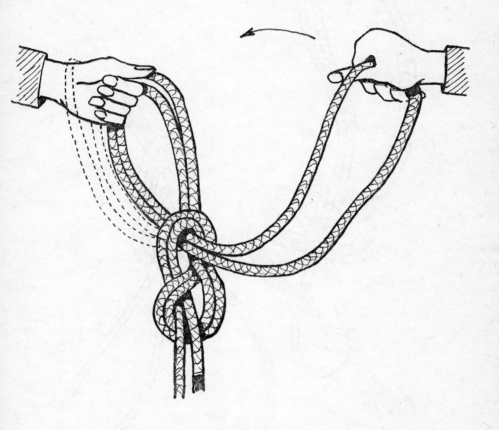

Fig. 53    Single rescue seat, step 4

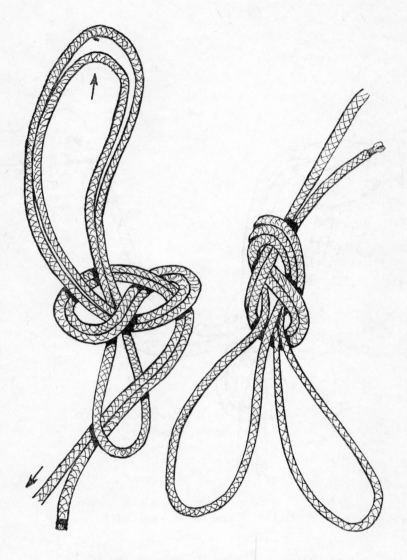

Fig 54   Single rescue seat, steps 5 and 6

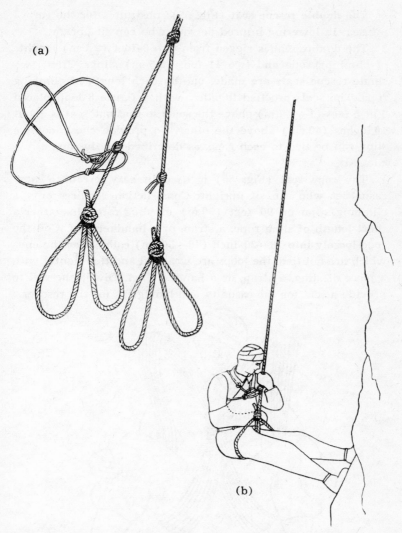

(a)

(b)

Fig. 55   (a) Double rescue seat with chest sling for casualty
          (b) Casualty being lowered in single rescue seat, secured
              by chest sling

The **double rescue seat** (Fig. 55) substitutes for the carrying seat in lowering injured persons who can sit upright.

The double seat is rigged from two 8-foot (2.5 m) lenghts of climbing rope and two 11-foot (3.5 m) slings. First, two single rescue seats are made, one on each length of climbing rope. The seats are tied together with a figure 8 loop placed 4 or 5 feet (1—1.5 m) above the seats so that one seat is about 16 inches (40 cm) above the other. To provide chest loops, a sling can be tied to each rope, as described for the single rescue seat.

The **rope seat** (Fig. 56) is used in easy terrain to carry casualties who can sit upright. Construction requires only a climbing rope or 90 feet (30 m) of sling rope plus either a short length of sling rope, a strap, or a handkerchief. Coil the rope loosely into 16—20-inch (40—50 cm) coils. Near the ends which are not tied, the loops are wrapped and tied tightly with a piece of sling, a strap, or a handkerchief. Divide the coil to provide a seat for the casualty and handgrips for the rescuer.

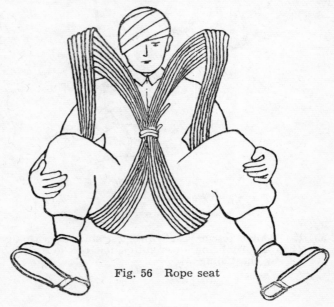

Fig. 56 Rope seat

# Rope Stretchers

The **interlaced rope stretcher** (Fig. 57) is employed to lower severely injured persons down difficult terrain. The rescuers can either use the loops for handholds or can run carrying poles through the loops.

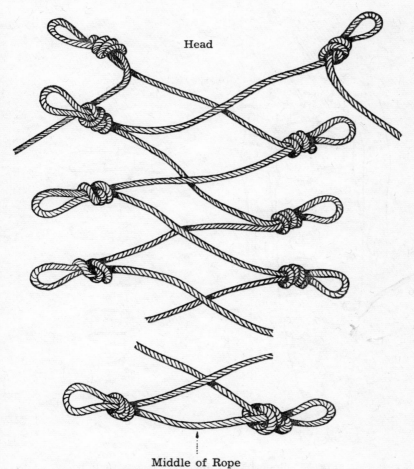

Head

Middle of Rope

Fig. 57  Rope stretcher, method of construction

Using a 100-foot (30 m) length of climbing or sling rope, tie two fistsize loops about 10 inches (25 mm) from the middle of the rope. Working out from these loops on each side tie three loops 20 inches (50 cm) apart, three loops 32 inches (80 cm) apart, and three loops 36 inches (90 cm) apart. Crisscross the

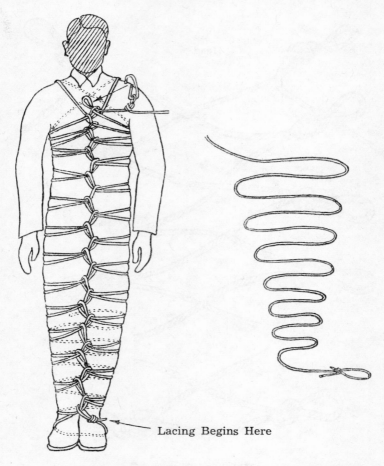

Lacing Begins Here

Fig. 58   Rope basket method of construction

92

rope so that the ten loops on each rope-half form a conically shaped net, leaving about six feet (1½ m) of free rope on either end.

The **rope basket** (Figs. 58—59) is the best substitute for the carrying sack in lowering injured persons. If a long, strong pole is available, the injured person can also be carried over a great distance by this method.

Tie a small fisherman's loop in the end of a 75- to 100-foot (25—30 m) length of climbing or sling rope. With the loop at the casualty's feet, lay out the rope in a narrow serpentine. Adjust the rope to body shape and length, using ample rope to

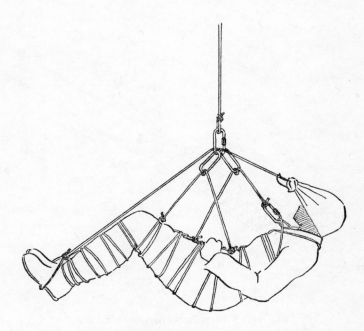

Fig. 59   Rope basket being used to lower casualty

93

keep the windings close together for body support. Place the injured person on the windings and pull them together, working up from the feet.

## Sleds

The **two-pole sled** (Figs. 60—62) substitutes for the mountain stretcher in easy terrain broken by slopes and ledges, the two soft branches acting as shock absorbers that ease travel for both casualty and rescuers.

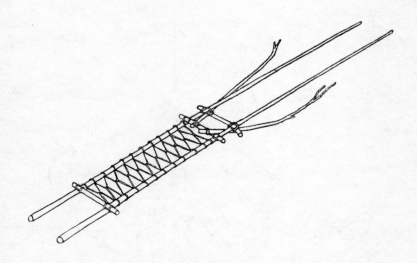

Fig. 60   Two-pole sled, over-all view

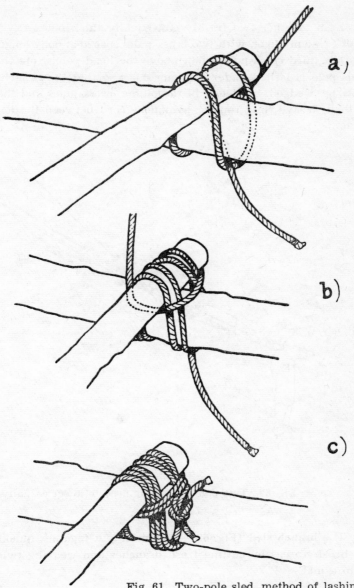

Fig. 61  Two-pole sled, method of lashing

Lash together two freshly cut, equally thick poles 13—16 feet (4—5 m) long, with two cross-poles spaced at body length. Lash a third cross-pole a foot above the head pole. Note that this pole is lashed *under* the long poles so that the branches can be wedged between the adjoining cross-poles and then lashed. Weave sling rope or avalanche cord between the long poles.

Fig. 62   Two-pole sled being used to lower casualty

The **branch sled** (Fig. 63—64) can be put together quickly in brushy areas by cutting fresh branches and weaving twigs into a mat.

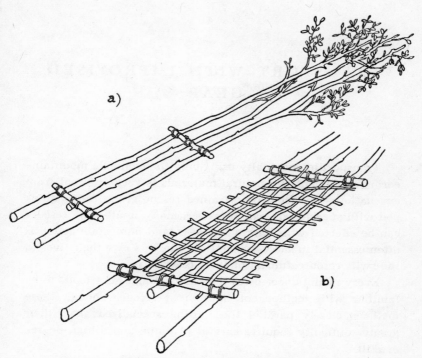

a)

b)

Fig. 64 Branch sled being used to lower casualty

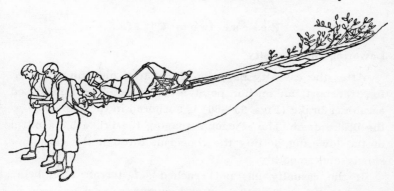

Fig. 63 Branch sled, method of construction

# \* 4

# TRANSPORT WITH IMPROVISED
# GEAR

Transporting a casualty using only the available mountaineering equipment and natural materials is very different from evacuations conducted by a trained rescue group fully equipped with specialized gear. However, many small-scale rescues can be effected with improvised gear, and immediate action is often essential to success; countless climbers owe their lives to the swift resourcefulness of their comrades.

Every mountaineer owes it to himself and his friends to be familiar with methods of improvised rescue. Though these methods closely parallel those using specialized gear, their greater difficulty requires careful planning and a high degree of skill.

## Rescue from Cliffs

### Lowering the Casualty

After the casualty has been given first aid and prepared for transport, an anchor point is prepared. The improvised **carabiner brake** (Figs. 65—66) is anchored in the same way as the brake drum. The rescuer managing the brake has control of the lowering, letting the rope run through the carabiner slowly and smoothly.

If the casualty has not reached safe terrain after being lowered one rope length, a second or even a third rope can be attached. With enough rope and enough manpower at hand, and with suitably steep and unbroken rock, a lowering sequence of as much as 300 to 400 feet (100—120 m) can be carried out from a single anchor point.

(a)                                                    (b)

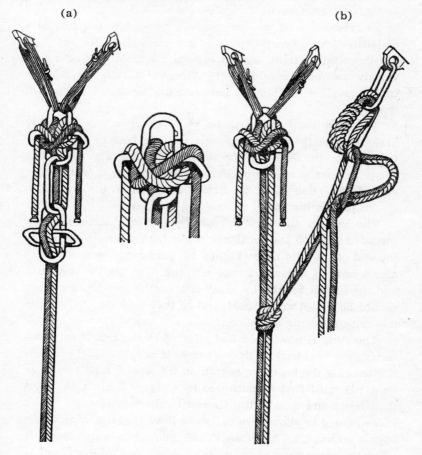

Fig. 65   Carabiner brake, anchor and rope details
         (a, b) Anchoring the lowering rope while adding a second
         rope to allow continued lowering

To add a second rope, the final foot of the first rope (single or doubled) is threaded through the carabiner in a figure 8 hitch (Fig. 65-a). *Under no circumstances should the rope be tied to the carabiner with a knot.* A prusik slings is then tied to the first rope about 12 inches (30 cm) below the carabiner brake (Fig. 65-b). If two persons are being lowered (casualty and attending rescuer), two slings are used. The sling, or slings, are then drawn tight, wound *around the solid side* of a previously anchored carabiner (1), threaded through the upper carabiner (2), and clamped between the tightened strands of the sling.

The first rope can now be removed from the carabiner brake — *slowly and kept under constant tension* — thereby tranferring the load to the anchored sling (Fig. 63-a). If a single rescuer is managing the entire lowering operation, the end of the sling must be firmly attached to the anchor, as shown to free his hands for the next procedures.

The end of the second rope (single or doubled) is now threaded through the carabiner brake far enough to be tied to the end of the first rope (Fig. 66-b), preferably with a fisherman's knot. If a doubled rope is being used for the lowering, and the cliff is broken by many ledges, the two joining knots should be a foot or so apart, rather than tied side by side, to minimize snagging on ledges.

The sling is now freed and allowed to slacken, thus transferring the load back to the carabiner brake. If a single rescuer is managing the lowering operation, the second rope (single or doubled) must first be anchored by a figure 8 hitch, the sling then freed and weight transferred to the second rope, which is then freed to allow resumption of lowering. If a second rescuer is on hand, he holds the Prusik knot open wide enough to allow the connecting knot and the second rope to slide through, thus saving much time and also providing an additional safety margin.

100

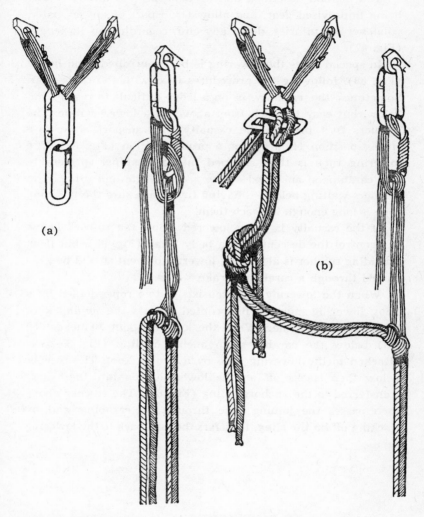

(a)

(b)

Fig. 66  Carabiner brake, anchor and rope details
(a, b) Anchoring the lowering rope while adding a second
rope to allow continued lowering

The method described above is the best of all those utilizing improvised gear, and allows transport of any casualty, whatever his injuries, down any cliff, regardless of its length (Fig. 67).

In special cases the lowering is best controlled from below (Fig. 68), following the procedures used with the cable gear. Sometimes the casualty is on a ledge difficult to reach from below, but easy to reach from above on a lowered rope. The rescuers first prepare the casualty for transport, either in a sitting position (Fig. 68) or a prone position (Fig. 69). The lowering rope is then snapped into a carabiner (preferably *two* carabiners) anchored at the accident site and dropped to rescuers waiting below — having first made sure the lowering rope is long enough to reach them.

If the casualty is being lowered alone, the rescuer below can control the descent with a body belay (Fig. 68), but if an attending rescuer is also being lowered, descent should be controlled through a carabiner brake.

When the lowering rope consists of two ropes joined by a knot, lowering must be interrupted to pass the joining knot through the carabiner. When the knot is about 20 inches (50 cm) below the carabiner, an anchored sling (Fig. 65-b) is attached to the lowering rope by a Prusik knot. The rescuer below then slacks off on the lowering rope until the load is transferred to the anchored sling (Fig. 68). The rescuer above then passes the joining rope through the carabiner and, by slacking off on the sling, transfers the load back to the lowering rope.

Fig. 67
Carabiner
brake being used to
lower casualty and
attending rescuer from
an upper station

103

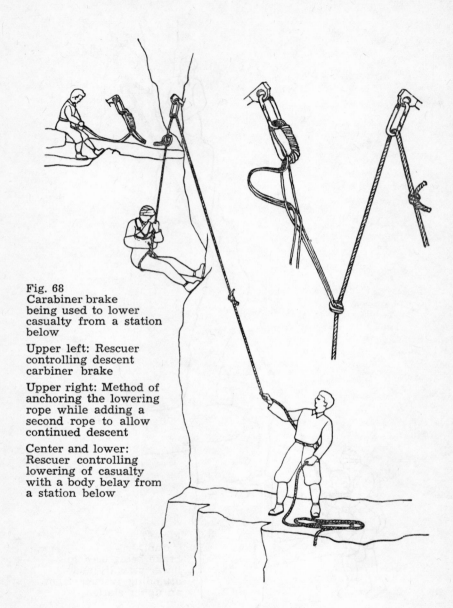

Fig. 68
Carabiner brake
being used to lower
casualty from a station
below

Upper left: Rescuer
controlling descent
carbiner brake

Upper right: Method of
anchoring the lowering
rope while adding a
second rope to allow
continued descent

Center and lower:
Rescuer controlling
lowering of casualty
with a body belay from
a station below

104

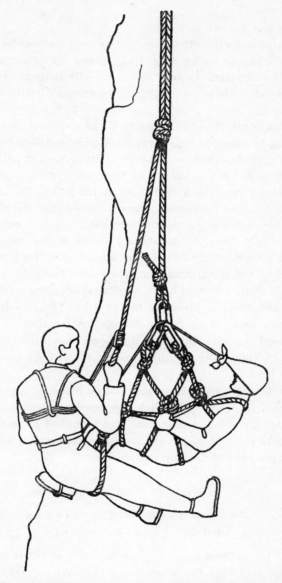

Fig. 69  Casualty being lowered in rope stretcher with **attending**
rescuer

## Hoisting the Casualty

The improvised method most often used for hoisting a casualty is the *single pulley* (Fig. 10-a). Since the effectiveness of the method derives merely from the elimination of friction encountered with a carabiner, the method is useful only for short hoists.

The rope carrying the casualty is snapped into an anchored carabiner (preferably *two* carabiners anchored side by side so that the rope passes through them easily). A short sling is tied with a Prusik knot to the leg of the rope leading to the casualty, making sure the knot is tied as far below the anchor as possible. Another carabiner is then snapped into the sling. The leg of the rope coming down from the anchored carabiner is snapped into the sling carabiner. To hoist the casualty, the rescuers then haul the rope in the direction of the arrow (Fig. 70-b) until the sling carabiner approaches the anchored carabiner. To allow a second hoist, another short sling coming from a separate piton is attached to the rope (Fig. 70-b) BY A *Bachmann knot*. With the Bachmann knot acting as a clutch to prevent back-slipping of the rope, the first sling and attaced carabiner can be slipped down toward the casualty for another haul.

*Translator's note: The double pulley provides a mechanical advantage. In recent years field use methods have been developed that promise to overcome the problems of friction and complexity which have, in the past, canceled out its theoretical advantages over the single pulley.*


## Rescue from Steep Slopes and Moderate Terrain

With improvised gear, as with specialized, often the major transport problems lie below the cliffs, on the steep, broken

106

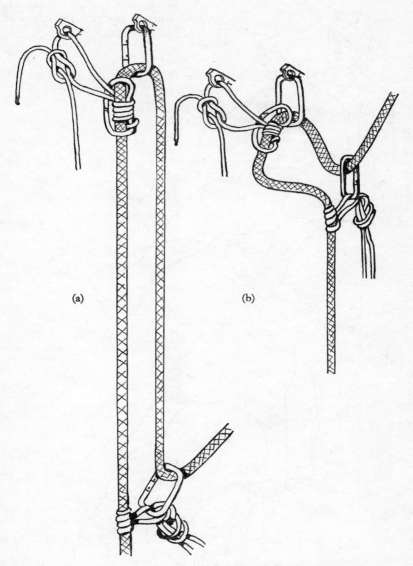

(a)

(b)

Fig. 70   Pulley arrangement used to hoist casualty

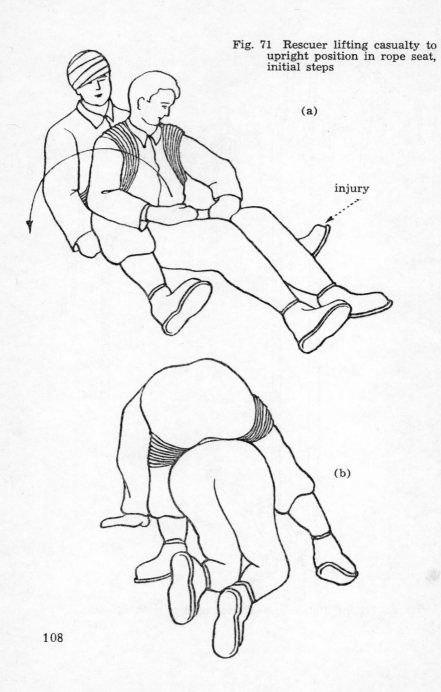

Fig. 71 Rescuer lifting casualty to
upright position in rope seat,
initial steps

(a)

injury

(b)

108

slopes where gravity no longer does most of the work, and where every motion sets loose shattered rocks that endanger both casualty and rescuers. In such terrain rescuers equipped only with normal climbing gear must depend principally on brute strength.

The best transport devices for most casualties are **sleds**. Among rock-strewn ledges and loose scree, special care must be taken to protect the casualty from falling rock. Transport should be conducted as much as possible in the fall line, avoiding traverses. On smooth slabs or steep meadows, the

(c)

Fig. 72    Rescuer lifting casualty to upright position in rope seat,
           final step

dragging requires little effort; indeed, the major consideration becomes control of the rate of descent. Depending on the amount of control needed, this may be done by installing a carabiner brake, setting up a body belay, or by tying two up-hill ropes to the sled, each controlled by a separate rescuer or set of rescuers.

The best transport device for casualties who can be moved in a sitting position is the **rope seat.** The sometimes difficult task of lifting the casualty into the seat can, with practice, be accomplished rather easily by using the illustrated method (Figs. 71—72). The casualty is lowered from the seat in exact reverse. In both cases the casualty should be turned so that his injury always faces outward from the slope.

On steep terrain the rescuer, carrying the casualty on his back, must be belayed (Fig. 73). Generally, he can best descend facing outward, using a long pole as a third leg to keep in balance. Upon encountering short vertical pitches, he should turn and back down while facing the wall.

Improvised stretchers are recommended only for terrain with a very moderate angle.

### Rescue from Crevasses

A team of three or four rescuers skilled in the previously described techniques of lowering and hoisting can evacuate a casualty from any crevasse, no matter how deep. In the exceptional case where cable gear is available, the methods are the same as those described for rock. Ordinarily, however, crevasse rescues are conducted using normal climbing equipment — rope, slings, carabiners, and ice axes.

**Pulley Method**

If the climber in the crevasse is injured, a rescuer must first descend to the casualty, render first aid, and tie him to the hoisting rope. On the surface, meanwhile, a pulley (Fig. 70) is

110

Fig. 73 Rescuer carrying casualty down steep slope in rope seat, belayed from upper stations

installed on one side of the crevasse (Fig. 74), anchored by several ice axes, ice pitons, or bollards. To reduce friction of rope against snow, the hoisting rope is held in the middle of the crevasse by a carabiner and sling anchored on the opposite

Fig. 74   Crevasse rescue: Pulley method

side. To prevent these ropes from trenching into the crevasse lips, they should run over ice axes or other gear anchored at the lips.

A single rescuer can do the hoisting while another rescuer shifts the Prusik knot — or preferably the Bachmann knot. When the casualty has been hoisted up to the suspended carabiner, the sling is slowly loosened, allowing him to be pulled over the crevasse lip.

## Stirrup Method

Almost invariably a crevasse rescue, to be successful, must be completed immediately after the fall; a human being cannot survive long in the hostile depths of a glacier, particularly if he is injured. It is essential, therefore, that every party venturing on a glacier be trained to carry out a swift, efficient crevasse rescue. To do so, both the person in the crevasse and those above must be the thorough masters of a proven method of crevasse evacuation. Though this is most notably true in the case of a small party, such as a single rope team, there is abundant recent evidence that numbers alone are no assurance of rescue success All too often an uninjured person has died hanging helplessly a few feet below the lip of a crevasse — while a few feet above him a large group of companions was helpless to save him. These numerous needless tragedies should be sufficient motivation for every glacier traveler to master the well-known stirrup method of rescue, and to be at all times prepared to use it.

The fundamental requirement for successful use of the stirrup (Bilgeri) method is advance preparation: every climber in a glacier party must be roped up correctly (Fig. 75). Each climber first rigs a chest harness and snaps it into a carabiner. A 100-foot (30 m) climbing rope is then laid out in three equal parts and the boundaries of the middle third marked with adhesive tape or some other device. For a two-man rope team, each of the two climbers then snaps his chest carabiner to a clove hitch tied in the climbing rope about 3 feet (1 m) toward the rope-end away from the tape marking the boundary of the middle third. The middle section of the rope, about 45 feet (15 m) in length, connects the two climbers during travel, and is thus their belay rope. The two end sections of the rope, each about 25 feet (15 m) long, are not used during travel, but are carried in reserve for rescue purposes. In some terrain the length of the belay rope can be even further reduced, providing even more reserve rope. Each climber ties a bowline foot-sling into the end of his reserve rope, then winds the reserve rope around his chest or stows it in his rucksack.

With a belay-rope length of 45 feet (15 m), a third climber, or even a fourth, can be added to the team. In ordinary crevasse travel, a middleman simply snaps his chest carabiner onto the belay rope so that it slides freely. Thus, a "sliding middleman" can alter the length of rope between himself and his team companions, allowing great flexibility in belayed travel through crevasses. However, in steep terrain each middleman must fix his chest carabiner in a static position on the rope, using a clove hitch.

The final preparation for glacier travel is for each climber to attach a rescue sling to the belay rope with a Prusik knot. This sling, which must be long enough so the climber can stand up in it comfortably, is *passed underneath the chest harness,* with the Prusik knot pushed close to the chest carabiner, and the sling stowed in a convenient pocket of the pants or coat.

Only with all these preparations completed in advance can the stirrup method be expected to be successful, particularly if a climber must be rescued from a crevasse by only a single companion. A team that ropes in this manner and takes care always to travel through crevassed areas with a taut rope will rarely suffer any injuries in a crevasse fall, and can thus ex-

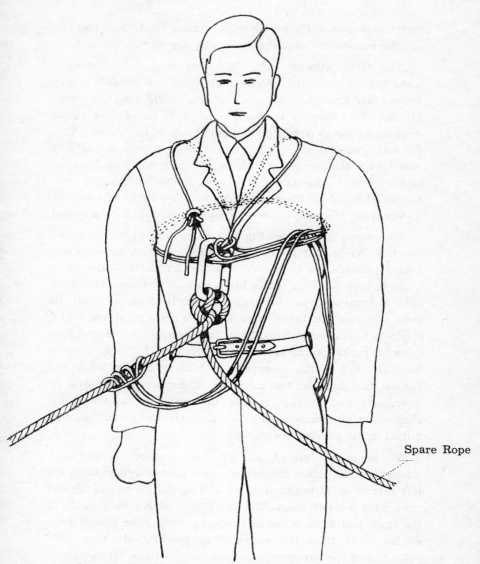

Spare Rope

Fig. 75  Crevasse rescue: Climber properly roped up in
preparation for stirrup method

115

pect the person in the crevasse to be fully capable of carrying out the maneuvers required of him by the stirrup method.

The fallen climber (Fig. 76), who may be dangling in midair, first pulls the rescue sling from his pocket, runs it *behind his knee and in front of his ankle over his instep,* all the while keeping his knee bent, then pushes the Prusik knot up as far as it will go and stands up in the stirrup. Thus his body weight comes off the cest harness into the stirrup, making his position sufficiently comfortable to await lowering of the reserve rope arrives, he runs it *underneath the chest harness,* behind his knee and in front of his ankle and over his instep. Now, standing in two stirrups, he is ready for the ascent.

His companion above (Fig. 77) must first, of course, arrest the fall. While still holding the fallen climber, by whatever means possible, he then drives his ice ax shaft as deeply as possible into the snow pulls his rescue sling from his pocket, frees it from his chest harness, and ties it to his ax shaft. He then unsnaps the belay rope from his chest carabiner and is ready to begin rescue operations. He removes the reserve rope from his rucksack and his chest harness from his body, ties the harness sling to the reserve rope with a Prusik knot, and fastens the sling to the ax shaft. The reserve rope, with its previously tied stirrup, is now thrown down to the fallen climber, who completes his preparations for ascent, as described in the previous paragraph.

To begin the ascent, the companion above calls *"left",* whereupon the fallen climber removes all his weight from the left stirrup by lifting his left leg and by pulling up on the left rope with his left hand. The companion above then hauls in the slack and anchors the left rope by sliding the Prusik knot as far away from the ax shaft as possible. He then calls *"right"* and the procedure is repeated until the fallen climber is able to scramble over the crevasse lip.

116

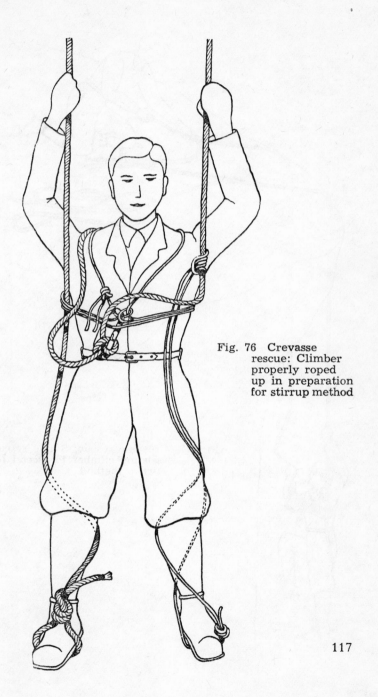

Fig. 76 Crevasse
    rescue: Climber
    properly roped
    up in preparation
    for stirrup method

117

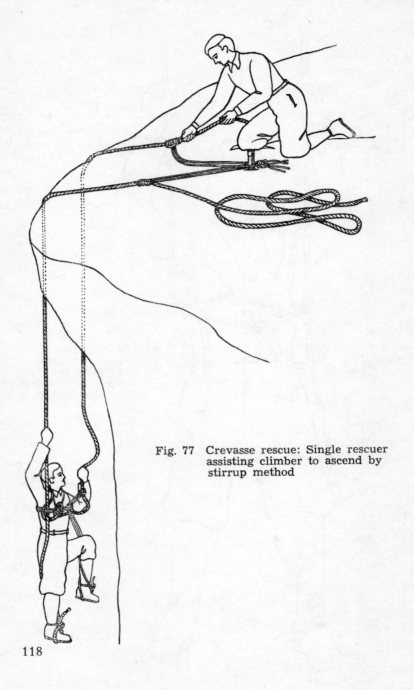

Fig. 77 Crevasse rescue: Single rescuer assisting climber to ascend by stirrup method

118

To prevent the belay and reserve ropes from trenching into the crevasse lip, and thus perhaps freezing solidly into the snow, they must be run over an ice ax shaft, crampons, a rucksack, or other gear placed close to the crevasse lip.

Rather obviously, the stirrup method is much simpler when two or more companions are above to share in the arrest and rescue. In this case each of the ropes can be controlled by a separate ax or body belay.

## Unaided Ascent

The **Prusik-sling method** of ascending a free-hanging rope, useful though it is to rock climbers, is rarely successful in crevasse rescue. Moving the stubborn knots along a wet or frozen rope often requires more strength than possessed by a fallen climber. Moreover, the rope may be trenched so deeply into the crevasse lip that at the end of his rope ascent the climber must somehow clamber up a vertical or overhanging wall many feet high.

A **newer stirrup method** is more helpful, though to use it the fallen climber must have two ice pitons, two carabiners, two slings, an ice hammer or ordinary piton hammer, and two short cords or crampon straps — plus considerable strength and a firm crevasse wall that will hold pitons.

The fallen climber (Fig. 78) ties a stirrup into each of his two slings and places one over each boot. He runs each sling underneath a cord or crampon strap tied around the leg below the knee. He ties three figure 8 loops into each sling, as follows: one just above the knee strap, one in the sling-end at the limit of easy reach, and one midway between the other two.

He then (Fig. 79) drives the first ice piton as high as he can reach, snaps a carabiner into it, and into the carabiner snaps the highest figure 8 loop of one of his slings. He drives a second piton, snaps in a second carabiner and the second sling.

Fig. 78  Crevasse rescue: Unaided ascent, initial step

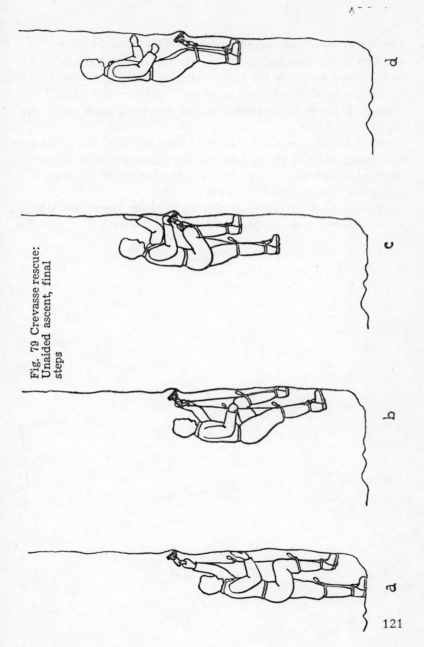

Fig. 79 Crevasse rescue:
Unaided ascent, final
steps

d

c

b

a

Then, placing all his weight on the second sling, he draws up the first sling (bending at the knee) until he can snap its second figure 8 loop into the first carabiner. Then, transfering all his weight to the first sling, he moves up the second sling. The procedure is repeated, removing and redriving each piton in turn.

To maintain a comfortable and stable position, the climber must keep the two pitons horizontally separated by a distance of several feet. Stability of stance is further aided by 12-point crampons that bite into the wall.

The climber trenches a passage through the crevasse lip while hanging from his highest pitons.

# PART TWO

# WINTER
# RESCUE

* 5

# SPECIALIZED WINTER RESCUE GEAR

Winter rescue consists mostly of transporting casualties from ski runs, and very rarely from snow-covered cliffs and ridges. Therefore, the most important winter transport device is a rescue sled. The ideal sled should have the following characteristics:

1. Slides easily on every surface from icy ruts to bottomless powder snow.

2. Slides both forward and backward.

3. Has a low center of gravity.

4. Is easily steered by means of a rigid connection between sled and rescuers.

5. Is lightweight and easily dismantled for carrying.

6. Is contour-fitted to the human body to allow full protection of the casualty from further injury and from the weather.

124

The most satisfactory sled, to date, is the boat sled **(akja)**, which can be used for any casualty in any condition of snow or ice, as well as below snowline. The **two-ski sled with ski-coupler,** though inferior to the akja, is far better than any other improvised sled.

## Akja

The akja (Fig. 80) has the shape and characteristics of a double-ended flat-bottom boat designed to "float" in the snow. For the sake of both hull protection and smooth sliding,

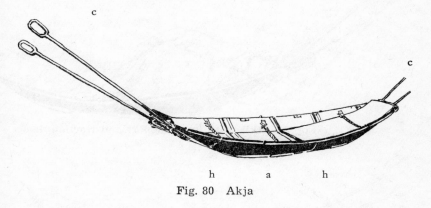

Fig. 80    Akja

two metal runners are fitted along the bottom edges (a) and one runner along each gunwale. For improved tracking on hard crusts, a pair of metal guides are attached to the front and back of the bottom runners (b). The steering handles (c), two at each end, are rigidly fastened but easily detachable. To cushion and insulate the casualty, the inside of the sled is covered with plastic-covered sponge-rubber mats.

The akja can be left permanently assembled at an alpine hut or rescue station, or taken apart into two sections for easy carrying on searches and expeditions. The tubular steel or aluminum handles may be one-piece, two-piece, or telescoped.

125

Akja hull, accessories, and handles together weigh from 24 to 30 pounds (12—15 kg).

The casualty must always be securely strapped to the akja. His injuries — which for obvious reasons are most commonly to the leg — can be splinted either with the leg support (Fig. 81) or with ski poles (Fig. 82).

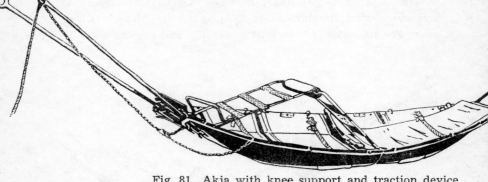

Fig. 81   Akja with knee support and traction device

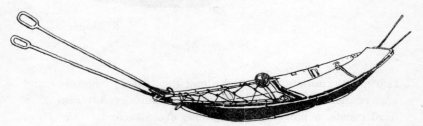

Fig. 82   Akja with ski poles improvised for splinting

Either identically shaped end of the akja can serve as the bow. Thus, rescuers never need swing-turn the akja into a new traverse, but can simply exchange stern for bow (Fig. 83). This ease in turning and changing direction is a major virtue of the akja, particularly on difficult snow or slope conditions and when being steered by unskilled skiers.

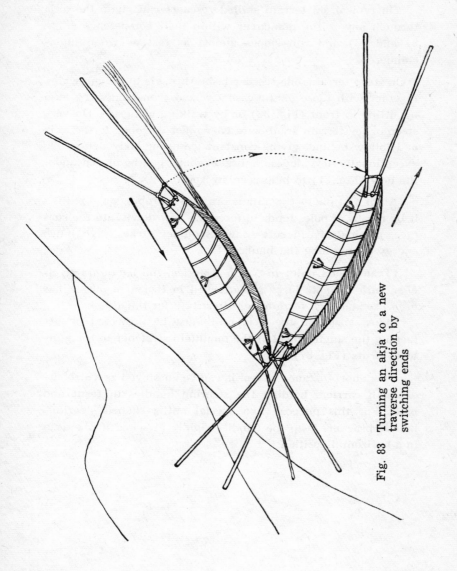

Fig. 83  Turning an akja to a new traverse direction by switching ends

On typical ski terrain skilled rescuers can guide the akja through any skiing maneuver within their competence (Figs. 84 and 85) and run slopes almost as fast as when unencumbered.

On steep terrain, one rescuer lashes his skis to the gunwales, together with those of the casualty, and then guides the akja by sitting in front (Fig. 86) or by walking alongside. On very steep or icy terrain another rescuer must be roped to the akja and follow behind, giving constant ice ax or body belays. On exceptionally icy slopes, a brake chain can be placed under the bow (Fig. 81) to help regulate speed.

Along flat plains the akja is dragged by ropes, since pulling it by means of poles tends to force the bow down into the surface, particularly in soft snow. Shoulder straps save much energy during long flat hauls.

(**Translator's note:** *In North America, the mountain stretcher with a single large ski attached in lieu of a wheel, has been used on such terrain as a substitute for the akja.*)

Below snowline the akja hull must be protected by attaching the single wheel of the mountain stretcher to the gunwale struts (Fig. 87).

Over short distances the akja can be employed as a stretcher, with carriers holding the steering handles in front and back. For this purpose two special antler-shaped steering-handle brackets keep the handles rigidly attached to the akja in a horizontal position.

128

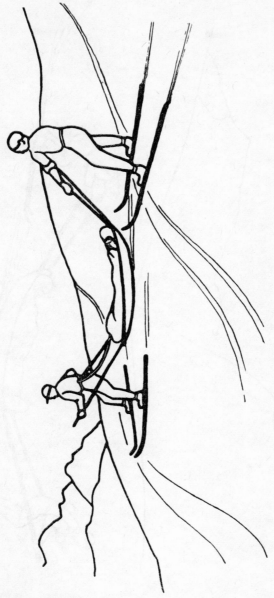

Fig. 84  Two rescuers guiding an akja

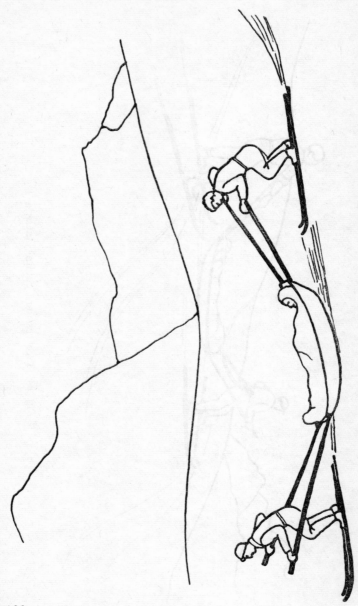

Fig. 85 Two rescuers guiding an akja

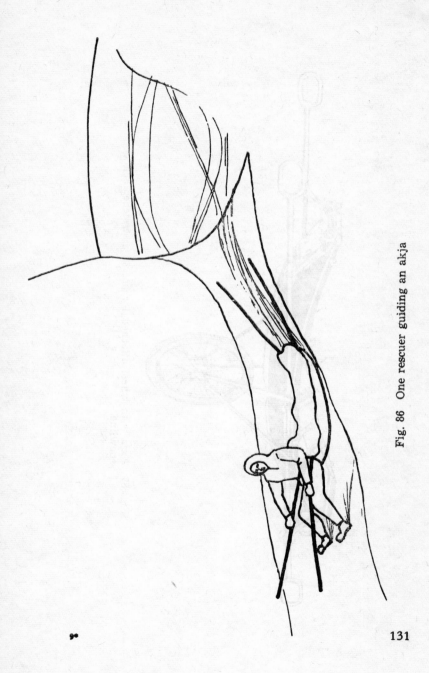

Fig. 86 One rescuer guiding an akja

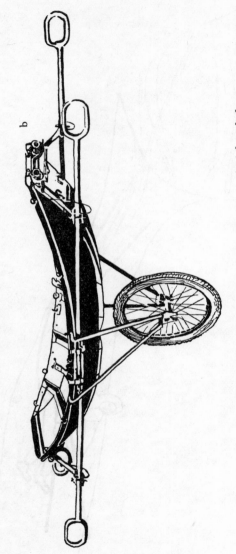

b

Fig. 87  Akja with wheel attached for use as a stretcher below
snowline

## Two-Ski Sled with Ski-Coupler

The two-ski sled with ski-coupler has the following components:

1. A ski-coupler (Fig. 88) composed of three parts: the front bar with two brackets tightened to the skis by

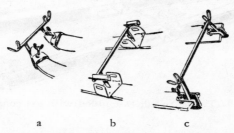

a      b      c

Fig. 88  Ski-coupler used for assembling two-ski sled

wingnuts; the middle bar and fastening attachments; the wingnut-tightened rear bar with keels for tracking in hard snow. The ski-coupler, made of thin steel tubes, weighs about 3 pounds (1.5 kg).

2. The casualty's skis and poles, one or two pairs of poles belonging to rescuers, two pairs of climbing skins, and a supply of slings or straps.

3. A canvas sack stretched between the skis to brace the sled and to insulate the casualty.

To construct the sled, first the skis are rigidly connected by means of the three parts of the coupler. The joined skis have somewhat the shape of a plough, their toes pointing slightly inward. Next the casualty's ski-pole handles are lashed to the forks of the rear coupling bar, with the pole wristloops (Fig. 89) and the pole points lashed inside the brackets of the middle coupling bar by means of slings or straps. Then the transport bed and cross-bracing are installed. This may be

133

done, if necessary, by weaving avalanche cord back and forth (Fig. 90). However the canvas sack is preferred if available.

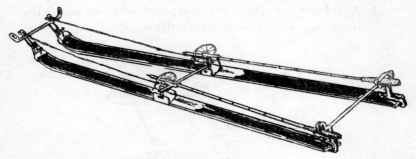

Fig. 89  Two-ski sled, assembled with ski-coupler

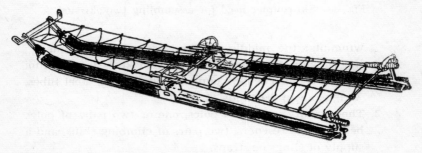

Fig. 90  Two-ski sled, cross-braced with avalanche cord as a bed
for the casualty

The sack is first tied to the rear coupler bar, tightened over the front bar until the skis bow rigidly upwards, and then is fastened to the bar; finally, cords sewn to the bottom of the canvas are stretched taut over the poles for cross-bracing (Fig. 91).

For travel through deep loose snow, two pairs of climbing skins are tied longitudinally under the sled to give a better sliding surface and to prevent snow from forcing up into the framework.

134

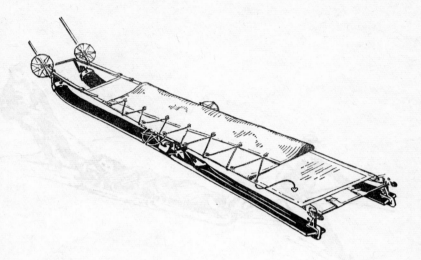

Fig. 91  Two-ski sled, with canvas bed for casualty

The sled is steered by means of rescuers' ski poles, or any available substitute, tightly lashed to the front and rear coupling bars (Fig. 92) or, in some situations, to the front bar only (Fig. 93).

For ease of handling, the casualty should ride feet first in deep snow, head first on packed slopes. This rule must be followed with any sled whenever swift transport is more important than medically ideal positioning.

On typical ski terrain, a pair of rescuers can guide the two-ski sled through all ordinary turns and maneuvers (Fig. 92). On traverses, one rescuer should travel below the sled, using his poles as levers to keep the rear from slipping (Fig. 93). A

Fig. 92  Two rescuers guiding a two-ski sled with poles

third rescuer, if available, can provide additional control by tying into the rear bar with a long avalanche cord and following behind.

On steep turns there should be a third rescuer below the sled to act as safety man in case of a fall. If two rescuers must negotiate a steep turn without help, they must bring the sled to a complete stop and then carefully pendulum the leading edge of the sled into the new direction.

Fig. 93 Single rescuer guiding a two-ski sled on a traverse, with a second rescuer preventing sideslipping

# 6

# IMPROVISED WINTER RESCUE GEAR

## Two-Ski Sled with Improvised Lashing

Every ski mountaineer should master the technique of assembling a two-ski sled with improvised materials and should always carry the necessary equipment in his rucksack. The two-ski sled is the only improvised sled that can be recommended for long hauls over every sort of slope and snow, particularly if the casualty has grave injuries. On easy terrain it can, in an emergency, be guided by a single rescuer.

The two-ski sled with improvised lashing (Fig. 94) is similar to the two-ski sled described in the previous chapter except that it is assembled using only the following equipment normally carried by ski mountaineers: the casualty's skis; two to four pairs of ski poles; three wooden crossbars, such as tree branches, each about 1-½ feet (40 cm) long; 6 feet (2 m) of sling rope or flexible wire; ski-repair screws, preferably of the Hummel design; an avalanche cord; two leather straps; one or two pairs of climbing skins.

To assemble the two-ski sled, the front and rear wooden crossbars are first lashed or screwed to the skis, which should be no more than 8 inches (20 cm) apart. Then the middle crossbar is tied to the ski bindings with leather straps, providing a base for the ski poles, which are also strapped to the bindings. Depending on the riding position selected for the casualty, the additional ski poles are lashed lengthwise either to the rear and middle crossbars, as illustrated, or to the middle and front crossbars. Next, to bow the skis upward, avalanche cord is stretched taut between the front and rear crossbars and looped over the middle crossbar for security. The re-

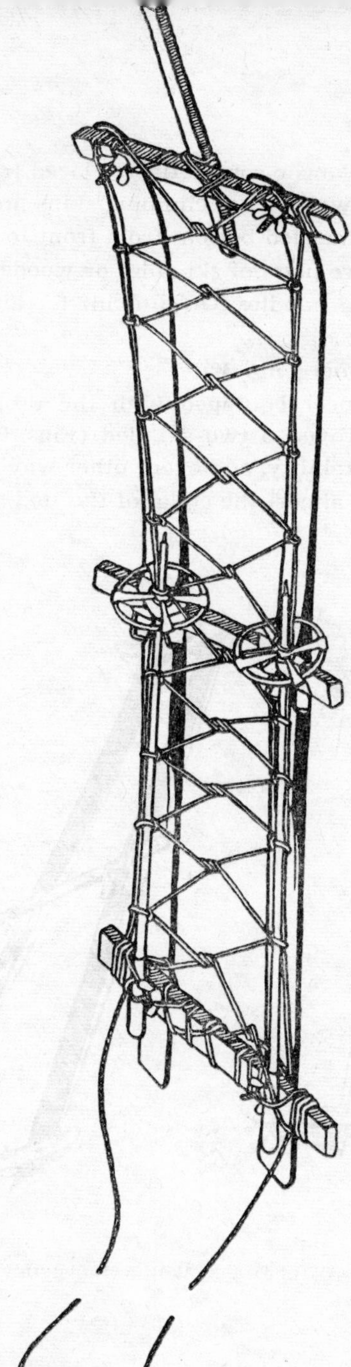

Fig. 94  Improvised two-ski sled

mainder of the avalanche cord is tightly laced from side to side for crossbracing. Two pairs of climbing skins are then stretched and tied along the sled bottom from front to rear crossbars. Finally, one or more pairs of ski poles or wooden poles are attached for carrying handles. On difficult terrain, a belay line should also be rigged.

**Variation Using Emergency Kit**

A ski mountaineer equipped with the proper emergency materials can improvise a two-ski sled (Figs. 95—97) that in maneuverability, stability, and every other way except comfort for the casualty, is almost the equal of the sled assembled with specialized gear.

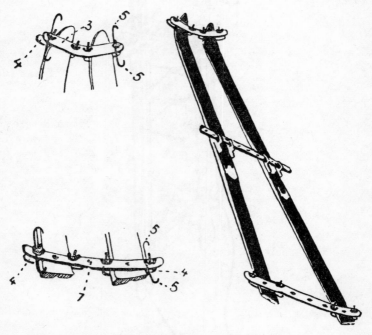

Fig. 95  Improvised two-ski sled using emergency kit, initial steps

The first requirement is one of the many modern rucksacks that has a framework containing from two to four removable aluminum slats. The second requirement is an emergency kit, weighing in all about 8 ounces (250 gr.), that contains the following: one aluminum slat about 10 inches (25 cm) long; four slats about 3-½ inches (9 cm) long; eight flathead bolts with wingnuts.

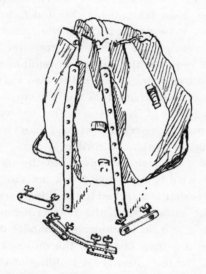

Fig. 96 Portions of rucksack used to improvise two-ski sled

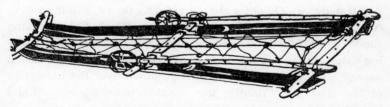

Fig. 97 Improvised two-ski sled using emergency kit, completed

141

Construction follows the principles previously described.

### Four-Ski Sled

The four-ski sled (Fig. 98) requires less equipment, time, and skill than the two-ski sled, and is thus a useful alternative where these considerations are important, particularly when the transport distance is short and the snow surface is hard. On every sort of terrain, its maneuverability is inferior to that of the two-ski sled. In deep snow it has two additional faults: first, one rescuer must take off his skis and flounder along on foot; and second, snow forces through the framework next to the casualty, increasing the danger of exposure.

Construction requires the following equipment: two pairs of skis; two or three pairs of ski poles; two curved crossbars (such as tree branches) about 1-½ feet (50 cm) long; between 6 and 10 feet (2—3 m) of sling rope or flexible wire or, preferably, some Hummel ski-repair screws; four leather straps; climbing skins or an avalanche cord.

If screws are used, a single hole is cut through each of the four ski tips; if wire is used, two holes are cut through each tip. The front crossbar is attached to the skis by screws or wires, and then, by the same means, the rear crossbar. To provide additional bracing, the ski bindings are connected with leather straps. Ski poles are then lashed to the outer skis to provide security railings for the casualty. A bedding of climbing skins or avalanche cord is prepared for the casualty at the front, as illustrated, if he will be riding head first; at the rear if he will be riding feet first. The steering handles are constructed as illustrated: two ski poles are individually thrust, handgrip first, through the baskets of the poles lashed to the sled, thus locking the steering poles to the railing poles; the baskets of the steering poles are then lashed to the wooden crossbar; next, a second pair of poles are thrust, basket first, down over the handgrips of the first pair; finally, the doubled poles are crossed and lashed together securely at the intersection.

142

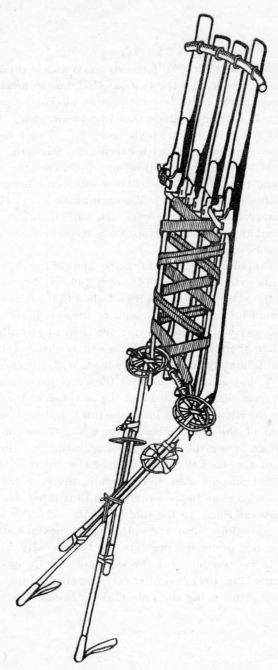

Fig. 98 Four-ski sled

143

## Two - Ski Drag

The two-ski drag (Fig. 99), formerly very widely used, has largely been superseded by the two-ski sled, but in level terrain and deep snow is still sometimes an alternative worth consideration. Its major virtue is that in an emergency it can be assembled and guided by a single rescuer — if that rescuer is an exceptionally fine skier with exceptional strength.

Construction requires the following equipment: the casualty's skis; one pair of ski poles; two wooden crossbars, such as tree branches or broken ski poles, each about 2 feet (50-60 cm) long; an avalanche cord; a rucksack stuffed full of gear; a pair of climbing skins, the straps of a second rucksack, or other suitable lashing material.

First the ski poles are lashed to the bottoms of the skis, with the pole points extending about 14 inches (40 cm) beyond the rear ends of the skis. The skis are then lashed to the rear crossbar with avalanche cord, the rear ends of the skis lying about 14 inches (40 cm) apart. The ski tips are then placed slightly closer together than the rear ends, about 12 inches (30 cm) apart, or approximately the length of a boot. With the skis thus spread in a V, but connected only at the rear, the avalanche cord is laced from rear to front. First, the cord marked with an arrow "a" in the illustration is laced the full length and used to lash one side of the front crossbar to a ski. Then the cord marked with an arrow "b" is interlaced with the first the full length and used to lash the other side of the crossbar to the other ski. For transport over steep terrain, the rear crossbar should be fastened close to the ski ends, as illustrated; on level terrain, somewhat closer to the middle of the skis. For cushioning, and sometimes also for splinting, a rucksack stuffed full of gear is tied under the bent knee of the casualty. To begin transport, the rescuer runs the ski pole tips through his rucksack straps (Fig. 100) or similar carrying straps improvised from climbing skins, using the pole baskets as handles.

144

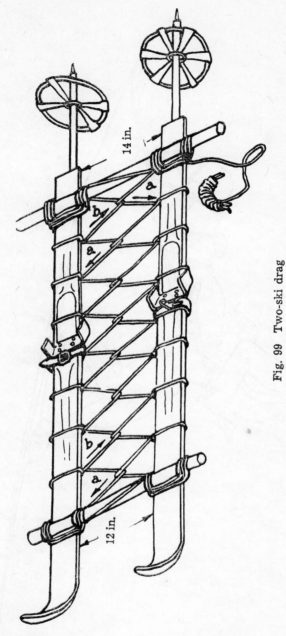

14 in.

12 in.

Fig. 99  Two-ski drag

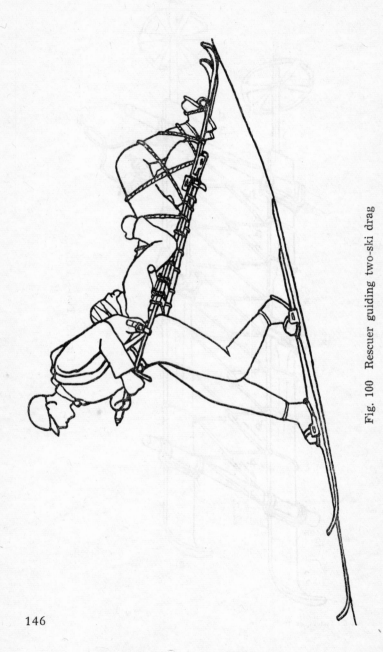

Fig. 100  Rescuer guiding two-ski drag

146

## Four-Ski Drag

The four-ski drag (Fig. 101) can only be used on trails and packed slopes where the rescuer can walk, but under such conditions it offers the casualty greater comfort than the two-ski drag and requires less muscular effort from a lone rescuer. On steep slopes a second rescuer must be available as a belayer.

Construction requires the following equipment: two pairs of skis; one pair of ski poles; three wooden crossbars, such as tree branches, from 1 to 2 feet (40—60 cm) long; between 6 and 9 feet (2—3 m) of sling rope or flexible wire, or preferably a ski-repair kit; avalanche cord; climbing skins.

First, a two-ski drag is assembled in the previously described manner, with the exception that the skis are placed closer together and no ski poles are attached. Next, the rear ends of the assembled skis are lashed to the bindings of the second pair of skis, the lashing method varying according to the design of the ski binding (Fig. 101-a). The tips of the second pair of skis are then connected with a wooden crossbar and the ski poles attached as illustrated (Fig. 101-b).

## Two-Ski Plough

Sleds of the plough design, whether two-ski or four-ski, require the least skill and construction time of any improvised sleds, but have very limited application.

The two-ski plough (Fig. 102) is useful for transporting casualties with minor injuries for short distances over easy terrain. It can be guided easily along the flat and down the fall line, but cannot be guided at all on traverses. The casualty ordinarily rides in a sitting position. The rescuer either walks or fashions extra-long handles and travels on skis.

Construction requires the following equipment: the casualty's skis; one or two pairs of ski poles; leather straps, or between 6 and 9 feet (2—3 m) of avalanche cord; a rucksack.

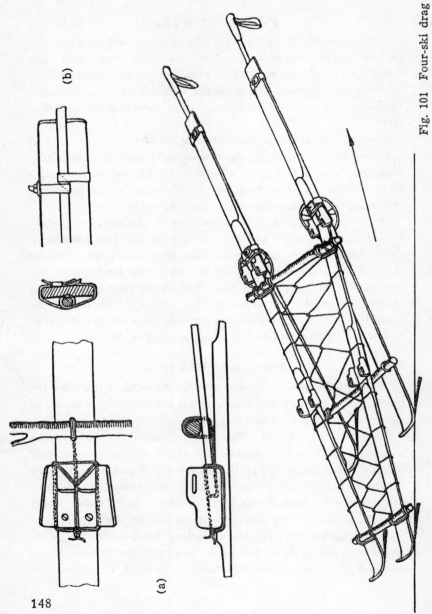

Fig. 101 Four-ski drag

(b)

(a)

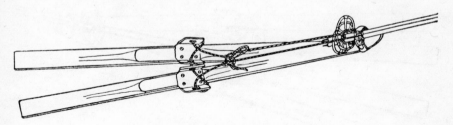

Fig. 102   Two-ski plough

The ski tips are crossed and tightly lashed together with straps or cord in a figure 8 pattern. At the same time, a pair of ski poles are tied to the crossed skis with the same lashing, in such a way that the baskets lie to the rear of the lashing and the pole handles to the front. If longer carrying handles are desired, a second pair of poles is tied to the first. The lashing cord is then tied to the bindings under tension. Finally, the bindings are tied together securely with straps or cord.

### Four-Ski Plough

The four-ski plough (Figs. 103 and 104) is particularly suitable for transport down steep slopes and on packed snow where the rescuer can walk. Depending on his injuries, the casualty rides either in a sitting (Fig. 105) or prone position.

Construction requires the following equipment: two pairs of skis; two pairs of ski poles; leather straps; between 6 and 9 feet (2—3 m) of sling rope or avalanche cord; one rucksack.

The tips of the four skis are crossed, with the rear ends diverging. Construction follows the principles described for the two-ski plough.

149

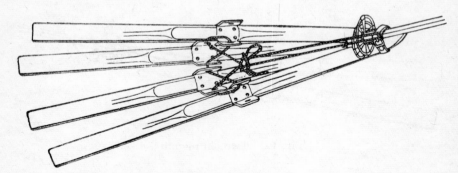

Fig. 103   Four-ski plough, over-all view

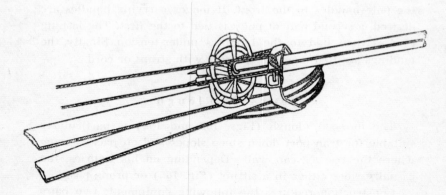

Fig. 104   Four-ski plough, lashing detail

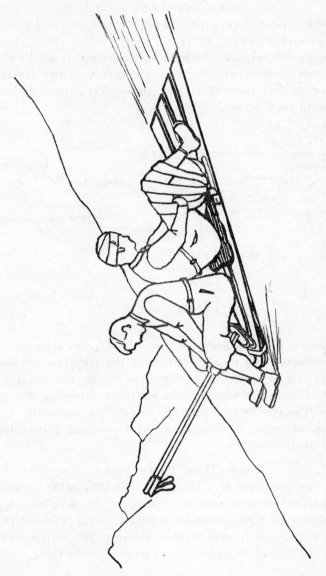

Fig. 105 Four-ski plough being guided by single rescuer

## Ski Stretcher

The ski stretcher (Fig. 106) is used in the same manner as any other stretcher (Fig. 107).

Construction requires the following equipment: one pair of skis or two wooden poles, such as tree branches; two jackets, coats, or parkas (anoraks); two rucksacks; some climbing skins, sling rope, or avalanche cord.

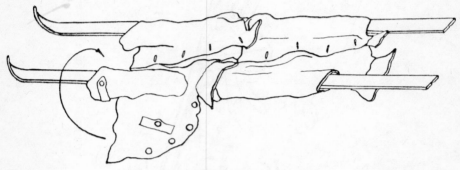

Fig. 106 Ski stretcher

If jackets or coats are used, the skis or poles are inserted into the sleeves and then the fronts of the jackets are folded over the skis or poles and buttoned. If parkas (anoraks) are used, the sleeves are turned inside out before inserting the skis or poles. The rescuers support the stretcher in part with their rucksack straps, as illustrated, or with climbing skins, sling rope, or avalanche cord.

## Two-Man Pole Seat

The two-man pole seat (Figs. 108 and 109) is the best device for transporting a casualty with minor injuries a considerable distance on foot, particularly when several teams of rescuers are available to take turns as carriers. The path must be wide enough to allow three men to travel side by side.

152

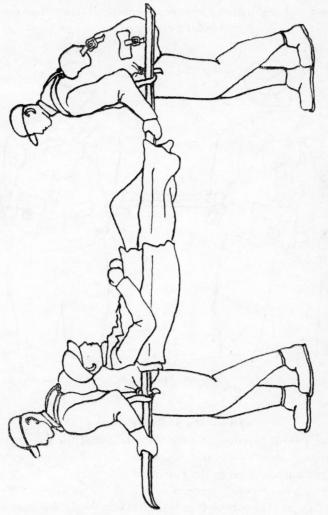

Fig. 107  Ski stretcher being carried

Two pairs of ski poles or tree branches are lashed together and inserted through the rescuers' rucksack straps. The carrying seat is padded with spare clothing.

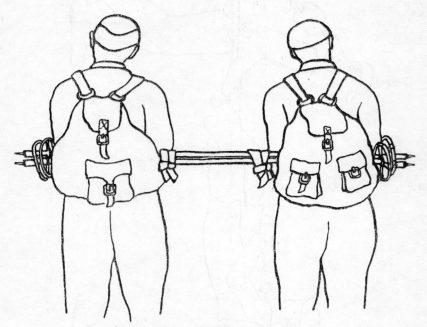

Fig. 108  Two-man pole seat, rear view

## One-Man Pole Seat

The one-man pole seat (Fig. 110) is useful for transporting a casualty with minor injuries a short distance, particularly over terrain unsuited to the two-man pole seat. The single rescuer must have great strength.

A pair of ski poles or tree branches are inserted through the rucksack straps, which must be reinforced with skins or cord. The rucksack must be empty or only partly filled with soft

Fig. 109  Two-man pole seat with casualty, front view

objects. The poles are padded with spare clothing. The casualty hooks his knees over the poles and wraps his arms around his carrier's neck.

### Rucksack Seat

The rucksack seat (Figs. 111 and 112) is an alternative to the one-man pole seat. An empty rucksack is slit open about a foot or so along the two side seams. The casualty dons the rucksack like a pair of trousers and is carried by one strong rescuer.

155

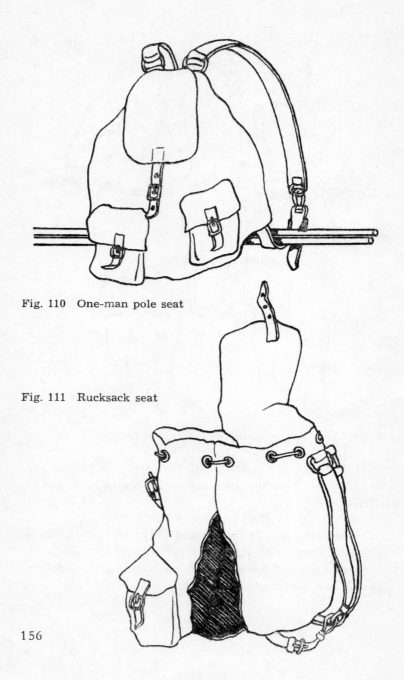

Fig. 110  One-man pole seat

Fig. 111  Rucksack seat

156

Fig. 112  Rucksack seat being used to carry casualty

# Splints

Since most winter rescues involve skiing casualties, and since many skiing accidents involve fractures, a knowledge of improvised splints is an essential part of every winter rescuer's background. For a full discussion of splints, the reader is referred to *first aid in alpine accidents,* by Dr. Hermann Angerer, published by the Oesterreichischer Alpenverein, and to *handbook of mountaineering medicine,* edited by Dr. James A. Wilkerson, scheduled for publication by The Mountaineers in 1965. The following paragraphs summarize the more important considerations involved in emergency splinting.

The upper extremities can generally be immobilized by materials carried by the party, such as gauze bandages, triangular bandages, or climbing skins. The casualty's own body can also sometimes be used, as in the case of splinting a fractured arm to the chest.

The lower extremities can usually be immobilized only with solid objects, such as ice axes, skis, ski poles, or any material found in the natural surroundings, such as tree branches. An excellent material for splints, and one frequently carried by ski mountaineers for emergencies, is corrugated cardboard, which has the additional advantage of providing insulation — though it must, of course, be kept dry.

Cardboard is the best material for immobilizing the lower leg (Fig. 113), but its use for immobilizing the upper thigh, pelvis, and back is highly questionable, and in any event requires several layers.

Another way to immobilize the lower leg and also the thigh is by means of two ski poles used in combination with a parka (anorak) (Fig. 114).

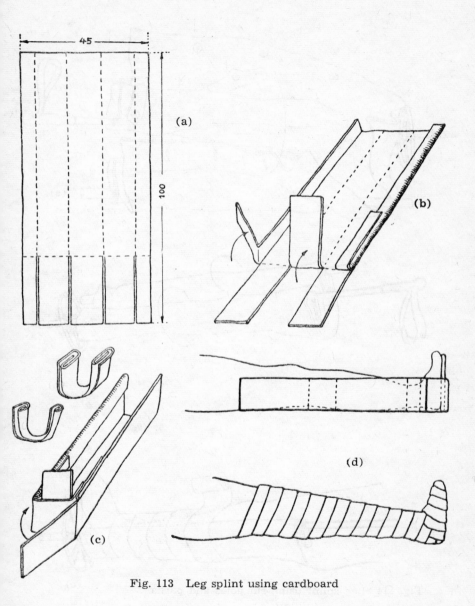

Fig. 113   Leg splint using cardboard

159

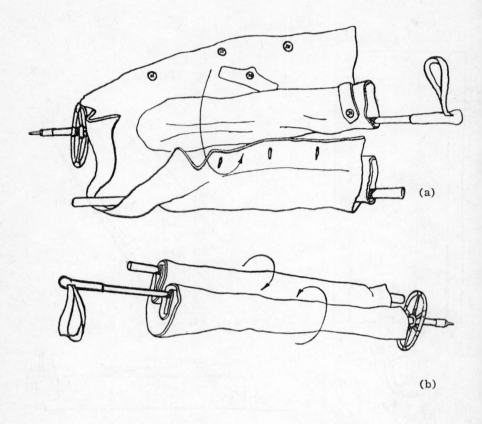

(a)

(b)

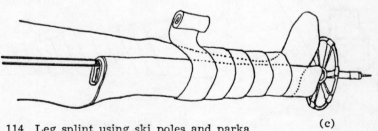

(c)

Fig. 114  Leg splint using ski poles and parka

160

The entire body can be immobilized temporarily by tying ski poles or ice axes from armpit to toes on each side of the body, with extra clothing added for padding, then lashing them together with avalanche cord, climbing skins, or triangular bandages.

One way to immobilize a fractured lower extremity is to use a traction splint, but this method should only be employed when it is necessary to alleviate pain so that a casualty can be transported a long distance using only the normal gear of a ski mountaineering party. *Traction can be used only when the casualty can be transported in the prone position.* Two ski poles or any similar splints are prepared a shown in Fig. 114-a. When the injured leg has been secured as shown in Fig. 114-b, a sling made of cord or belt is wound around the ankle, crossed over the forefoot, and the ends tied together underneath the sole. Next another cord, 12 inches (30 cm) long, is stretched between the knot underneath the sole and the protruding end of a pole. Then a short stick is inserted in this sling as a lever and traction is gradually applied by slowly twisting the stick. *The minimum amount of traction needed to provide relief from pain is the maximum permissible degree of traction.* Any greater degree of traction may allow muscles and tendons to slide between the bone fragments. Once traction is complete, the twisting stick must be secured and transport can then begin. *Traction must never be used on the arms: Permanent damage can be caused by injuring the radial nerve.*

# 7

# AVALANCHE RESCUE

Information received at the rescue base concerning the location and extent of an avalanche determines the detailed planning of a rescue mission, but the rescue leader, in general, follows the procedures described below.

A team accompanied by an avalanche dog has the best chance of success. If avalanche dogs are available, one or several dogs and their keeper, together with two to four rescuers and a doctor, should depart for the accident scene without delay. When dogs are used, rescuers should, if possible, avoid setting foot upon the search area.

The rescuers should carry avalanche probes, cords, and shovels. The doctor should carry an adult-size and a child-size Resuscitube for mouth-to-mouth artificial respiration and drugs for influencing the circulatory and respiratory systems.

The follow-up team of rescuers, whose number depends on the number of victims buried and also on the size of the avalanche, should carry avalanche probes, cords, shovels, first aid equipment, blankets, warm clothing, food, liquids, and lights — preferably searchlights.

On arriving at the avalanche site, the leader should inform himself of steps taken by those already on the scene, and then, based on his own survey of the situation, plan subsequent operations — taking into particular account the safety of the rescue team itself.

To prevent disaster from subsequent avalanches, warning guards must be posted immediately (Fig. 115). Next, the

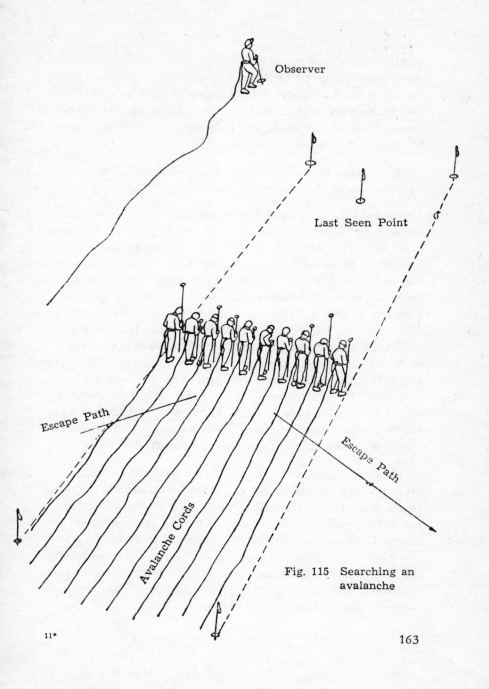

Observer

Last Seen Point

Escape Path

Escape Path

Avalanche Cords

Fig. 115  Searching an
avalanche

general area where the victim was last seen (and thus where he is most likely to be found) is examined by the "hasty search" method — preferably by dogs and their keepers. After this preliminary search, the dogs are spaced out for a more thorough search, a technique which should only be attempted by keepers with special training.

If no dogs are available, human rescuers carry out the hasty search and, immediately thereafter, begin probing.

The probing team should be stationed in a single line, horizontally across the lowest extent of the avalanche, one step apart from each other. The team then moves uphill along the avalanche, on signal from the leader. Each rescuer probes his assigned area down to the full length of the probing pole. If the probe encounters mild resistance, it is rotated under slight pressure so that parts of the buried person's clothing may adhere to the barbed hook. Whether or not this confirming evidence is gained, digging must begin immediately at the point of resistance. Probing should be done with particular care below ledges, in gullies, near trees and rock outcrops, and also wherever the avalanche forks or bends. Markers should be placed to indicate areas probed. If there is any further avalanche danger, rescuers should wear avalanche cords and always keep in mind their proper escape route.

If probing is of no avail, and if the avalanche depth is so great that the bottom cannot be reached with probes, the avalanche must be trenched all the way from its lowest extent to the point where the victim was last seen. Depending on the depth of the avalanche, the trenches should be from 3 to 5 feet (1—2 m) wide. Depth and spacing of the trenches depends on the thickness of the avalanche snow that cannot be reached by probing. Within the trenches, probing is carried out perpendicularly and obliquely in all directions.

Detailed instructions concerning avalanche rescue and first aid for avalanche victims are given in the *Avalanche Manual for mountain rescue teams,* by Albert Gayl, published by the Federal Union Of The Austrian Mountain Rescue Service, and in the *Avalanche Handbook,* published by the United States Forest Service, U. S. Governement Printing Office, Washington 25, D. C., U. S. A.

# WINTER TRANSPORT

Winter transport in steep alpine terrain employs the same methods as summer transport, but winter conditions add greatly to the difficulty and place much higher demands on the rescue teams and their equipment. The first requisite to success of a winter rescue is protection, both of the casualty and the rescuers, from the cold; such protection is provided by proper personal clothing, tents, sleeping bags, and stoves for preparing hot beverages. Protection of the casualty from effects of exposure and shock is even more urgent than in summer rescues.

Lowering a casualty down cliffs with climbing ropes presents greater difficulties than in summer, since the ropes become wet and icy. Cable gear, on the other hand, can be used in winter almost as easily as in summer. The carrying sack is used more frequently for transport of seriously injured persons, supplemented by blankets or sleeping bags The akja is used more often for lowering down steep slopes and gullies, particularly when the snow is hard.

When sufficient steel cable is available, a single lowering sequence may cover as much as 1000 feet (300 m); otherwise, lowering should be done in successive stages. Depending on snow conditions, one or more ice axes or skis may be used to construct an anchor.

If only two ordinary climbing ropes are available, both ropes should be tied to the sled and the casualty lowered in stages (Fig. 116), anchored by axes or skis; for particularly steep stretches, the carabiner brake should be used. If a brake chain is not available, a twisted rope tied to the sled at right angles to the line of descent serves as a effective brake.

Should it be necessary to transport a casualty uphill, the sled can be hoisted, one rope length at a time, by two to five rescuers. Depending on the snow conditions and the terrain, one or more rescuers must be available to lift the sled in front, and brace it at the rear, to prevent the load from slipping downhill during the intervals between hoisting (Fig. 117). On very steep slopes, a set of pulleys facilitates uphill transport.

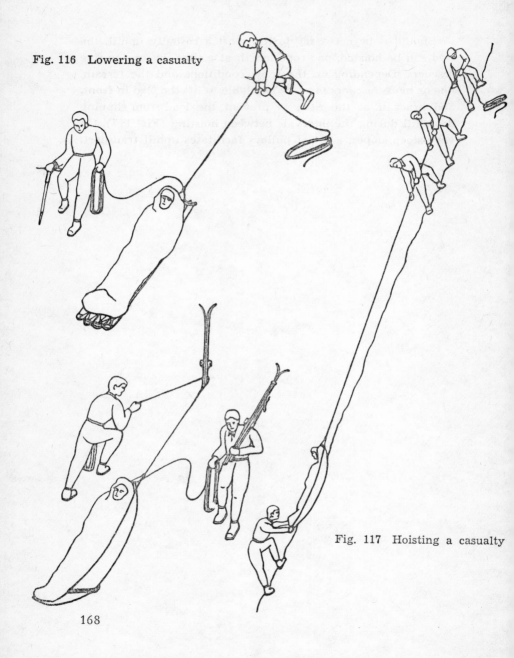

Fig. 116  Lowering a casualty

Fig. 117  Hoisting a casualty

168

# PRINCIPLES OF FIRST AID
# FOR MOUNTAINEERS

This outline should not be considered
a substitute for a thorough training in first aid
conducted by qualified instructors.

| INJURY | CAUSE | SYMPTOMS |
|---|---|---|
| All injuries and sickness:<br>1. General directions | Various | Various |
| All injuries and sickness:<br>2. Transport directions | Various | Various |
| Shock | Extensive hemorrhage; fractures; severe blows to the chest, abdomen, or kidney region; limb strangulation (caused by suspension from rope); burns; frostbite; fear; anxiety; or severe pain. Shock may be intensified by exertion, exposure, hunger or thirst. | Patient's skin is pale gray and covered with cold sweat. Pulse is fast, breathing is shallow, lips and nose are blue. No vomiting occurs. Patient is thirsty, feels cold, shivers (has goose pimples), and has dilated pupils. At first patient is conscious and restlessly nervous. Later, he becomes sleepy, slowly |

170

Keep the patient prone, quiet, and warm. Preservation of body temperature is of paramount importance, as the ability of the victim to maintain his normal temperature decreases rapidly in direct proportion to the outside temperature and to the severity of his injuries or illness. External heat must be provided when patient is in shock. If surgery is anticipated, the patient must not be allowed to eat, since an empty stomach is a prerequisite to a general anesthesia. The patient may have light food and liquids only if surgery is definitely not anticipated. Tea, coffee, lemonade, or fruit juices are preferable to water. Aspirin is valuable to relieve fever as well as pain. Give the patient ample opportunity to relieve himself before transport is started.

Plan transport details as thoroughly as time allows. The patient should be secured properly at the beginning of the trip to minimize discomfort from shifting. Warmth is essential and, since a patient in shock does not produce sufficient body heat, external heat may be required. Prior to transport, heat sources may be fires, portable heaters, propane-gas infra-red radiation heaters, hot water bottles, etc. During transport, hot water bottles or chemical heatpads should be placed on both sides of the patient within a pre-warmed sleeping bag. Accident victims tolerate cold poorly, so watch for frostbite signs.
There are some special cases in which the need for speed precludes time-consuming efforts to warm the patient: (1) Where brain injury is suspected, haste is imperative, but the patient should not be jarred. (2) Speed is also imperative for cases involving severe abdominal pain, which may indicate appendicitis, peritonitis, strangulated hernia. (3) Speed may be life-saving in cases of internal bleeding within any body cavity.

Keep the patient dry and warm. If shock is severe, and intravenous blood-expanders are not available, temporarily elevate and bandage the uninjured limbs, starting at the feet and hands and working toward the hips and shoulders, to move venous surface blood toward the heart as so-called "auto-transfusion." Absolute rest and gentle care are the best treatment. Give small amounts of sugar in hot tea or coffee, along with sedatives or pain killers. If it becomes necessary to transport the patient, extreme care and frequent stops are essential. Watch for acceleration of shock symptoms while en route and stop for treatment if they appear. **Always give preventive first aid for shock, regardless of symptoms.**

171

| INJURY | CAUSE | SYMPTOMS |
|---|---|---|
| | | loses consciousness, and finally goes into a deep coma as a prelude to death. |
| Unconsciousness | Various illnesses, or blow to the head | Any condition resembling death, yet without final confirmation of death — after a critically precise examination reveals that not all symptoms of death (as described at the end of this chapter) definitely are present. |
| Wounds: 1. Blood oozing | Laceration or cut | Steady oozing from numerous small blood vessels. Easy to recognize after pressing dry, sterile dressing momentarily and removing it for inspection of the wound. Depth and size of wound are of minor importance. |
| Wounds (cont.): 2. Venous bleeding | Laceration or cut | Steady flow of dark blood welling up continuously within small area of wound. Firm pressure stops bleeding, but moderate pressure increases flow. |

Make certain that air passages are unimpeded by vomit, sand, dirt, snow, or other blocks. Remove any removable false teeth. Check first for neck injuries and, if present, splint neck along its back before moving the patient, then turn him on his side to allow drainage from mouth and nose. Keep him warm and dry, and do not give him food or liquids while he is unconscious. Apply mouth-to-mouth breathing if respiration fails. If the heart stops, apply external heart massage as follows: Place the patient on his back over a firm support; with the heel of one hand (and with the other hand placed crosswise on top of it) press the lower third of the patient's breastbone forcefully toward the spine, about once per second. A second man should be present to apply mouth-to-mouth breathing in a rhythm of 16 times per minute. He should extend the victim's neck and pull his tongue out to keep the air passage open. If a second person is unavailable, the rescuer must interrupt the heart massage every 30 seconds to give a few breaths of artificial respiration. These efforts must be continued until a physician is present or until futility becomes evident after one hour of work.

Do not touch or wash wounds except to remove clearly visible foreign objects such as wood, stones, or bits of clothing. Clean area around wound and apply sterile dressings, using mild pressure. Beware of tight bandages, especially when left on for hours. The damage to the circulation caused by excessively tight bandages may be worse than the wound itself.

Using firm pressure, apply a sterile dressing directly over the source of the blood flow. If the bleeding originates deep inside the wound, pack the wound with sterile dressings. Keep a count of such dressings, mark the number down, and inform the doctor about them. Elevate bleeding limbs above the height of the heart. Never use a tourniquet to stop venous bleeding.

| INJURY | CAUSE | SYMPTOMS |
|---|---|---|
| Wounds (cont.) 3. **Arterial bleeding** | Laceration or cut (Wound may be superficial; depth is immaterial) | Blood spurts with pulse rhythm and is bright red. Spurting does not stop until artery is pressed firmly against bone or is clamped, preferably with sterile surgical forceps, and then tied with a string. Moderate compression will first slow the bleeding, then increase it as the artery continues to spurt under blood clots. |
| Wounds (cont.): 4. **Open, fresh** | Laceration or cut | Bleeding may be minimal, therefore presenting a minor problem only. Muscles tendons, nerves, bones may be exposed and thus may become infected. There is pain, although it may be absent in the beginning. |
| Wounds (cont.) 5. **Open, old, inflamed, infected** | Laceration or cut, then contamination with dirt or bacteria | Reddening and swelling accompanied by pain and localized heat. Area may throb, and general fever begins after some time has elapsed. There may be painful lymph nodes under the armpit or in the groin if the wound is on the arm or the leg, respectively. |

Firmly apply a sterile dressing directly over the artery. If firm pressure toward the bone does not stop the spurting, grasp the artery with your fingers and, keeping them in the wound, stuff sterile dressing around your fingers. Have a bandage applied around the patient's wound and your hand, until medical attention (surgical clamps, blood replacement, or blood-expanders) is available. Disregard the obvious risk of wound infection, since the patient's life is dependent on stopping the loss of blood. Only if all this fails, apply a broad tourniquet as firmly as necessary to stop the spurting between the bleeding point and the heart. In the field, a tourniquet must never be allowed to remain in place longer than one hour continuously. At intervals of less than an hour, the tourniquet must be released for ten minutes while someone applies firm pressure with sterile dressings over the bleeding point. Elastic bandages, neckties, belts, or suspenders may be used as a tourniquet, but never ropes, cords, or wires. The extreme danger to the limb by the application of the tourniquet increases drastically with decreasing outside temperatures; in temperatures below 32° F (0° C) a tourniquet may be applied for a few minutes only, in order to permit grasping the spurting blood vessel with the fingers.

Cover the wound with a sterile dressing after gross particles have been removed. Cleanse skin around the wound with water or snow, and soap if available. Apply ample dressing using slight pressure.

Elevate and immobilize the infected area. Apply moistened packs locally. For moistening, use alcohol, water, aluminum acetate (Burow's solution, in the ratio of one part to ten parts sterile water — never use undiluted) or potassium permanganate solution in the ratio of one 0.5-gram tablet to one quart or 250 cc (8 oz.) water, preferably as hot as can be tolerated. Use cold water only if hot water is unavailable. Apply plastic bag over the moistened packs to prevent evaporation.

| INJURY | CAUSE | SYMPTOMS |
|---|---|---|
| Bruises without surface wounds (Hematoma) | Violent external force to joints or soft tissue | Pain and swelling; subsequent bluish bruises on the skin. |
| Inflamed wounds, abcesses, furuncles, skin infections | Contamination, scratching, inadequate first aid | On arms, red lines running to armpits; on legs, running to groin. ("Blood poisoning" is actually lymphangitis, with inflammation of lymph glands.) |
| Large furuncles or carbuncles (combined furuncles and boils) | Localized skin infection | On back of neck whole area may become hard, causing extreme pain, fever, and a stiff neck. Boils on extremities may cause red lines as described above. |
| Inflamed toes and heels, blisters, sore toenails | Foot rubbing on boot or unmended sock | Patient limps. Affected areas are red and swollen, sometimes with blisters. |
| Recent insect stings, tick bites, spider bites | The obvious cause may often be found in retrospect | Area is swollen white or red, and is accompanied by pain and later itching. Many stings may cause general swelling. Ticks may be found on exposed parts of the body, often under hair. Ticks in back of neck may cause general paralysis, but full recovery will result after tick has been removed. |

# FIRST AID

Elevate the bruised area if possible. Apply cold packs with one part aluminum acetate (Burow's solution) to ten parts sterile (boiled) water; or use plain water. Immobilize the area if possible.

Immobilize the patient and apply packs moistened with 1 : 10 solution of aluminum acetate (Burow's solution). Use sterile (boiled) water if possible, as hot as can be tolerated. After applying packs, wrap a plastic bag over them, to prevent evaporation.

Make a ½-inch deep cut with a knife or razor blade (sterilized by holding in a flame) in the furuncle to drain pus, and apply a sterile band-aid or compress.

Protect the painful area with cotton gauze or felt padding. Open the blister with a needle sterilized in a flame and apply a sterile band aid or compress.

Remove the stinger if possible. Do not contaminate by scratching. Take antihistamine tablets and apply antihistamine ointment. Apply moist cold packs to the swollen area. Drop alcohol or tobacco juice on ticks; do not tear body of tick from its head which is imbedded in the skin.

| INJURY | CAUSE | SYMPTOMS |
|---|---|---|
| Fractures:<br>1. General prin-<br>ciples:<br>a. Simple:<br>   including<br>   comminuted<br>   (more<br>   than two<br>   fragments of<br>   bone); skin<br>   unbroken | Falls, blows from<br>falling objects, twists,<br>slips | Any or all of the<br>following may be<br>found: inability to use<br>the limb, displacement,<br>shortening, localized<br>pain on pressure of<br>the limb or on motion<br>of the ends towards<br>each other, gradual<br>setting-in of blood<br>effusion, abnormal<br>passive mobility,<br>grating of bone ends. |
| b. Compound<br>   skin:<br>   pierced by<br>   bone fragment | Falls, blows from<br>falling objects, twists,<br>slips | Skin penetrated from<br>within by bone frag-<br>ments, or from with-<br>out by force of im-<br>pact. Bone ends may<br>be visible. |
| 2. Special types:<br>a. Skull<br>   (see also **head<br>   injuries**) | Impact | Bleeding from wound<br>or from ears, nose, or<br>mouth; but bleeding<br>may be absent. Blood<br>rings may appear<br>around the eyes after<br>24 hours.<br>Brain damage may be<br>present if any vital<br>physical or mental<br>function appears<br>disturbed. |
| b. Neck | Direct fall on head or<br>neck. (Any injury to<br>the skull may injure<br>the neck too) | Patient desires to<br>keep neck immobi-<br>lized. Neck is painful<br>to the touch or on<br>pressure applied to<br>the top of the head. |

Immobilize the limb by splinting (including both adjacent joints), using plywood, sheet metal, boards, sticks, etc. Preferably, straighten the limb to near normal position to ease pain. Use plenty of padding for cushioning, and elevate the limb if possible. Use traction only as a last resort. Replace wet clothing with dry, or use blankets. Loosen shoelaces and any tight bandages to prevent cutting off circulation, which could cause permanent circulatory damage.

Apply a sterile dressing, and splint without attempting to straighten the limb. Do not use traction or attempt to get bone ends under the skin. If the bone ends do slip back under the skin, as often ocurs, notify the doctor that the wound is contaminated.

The severity of this injury demands quick, careful transport. Keep the head slightly higher than the heart and stop the outside bleeding with a head compression bandage.

Avoid any forward or sideways bending of the head by placing a rigid splint vertically at the back of the head and neck and bandaging or taping it securely to forehead and chest.

12*

| INJURY | CAUSE | SYMPTOMS |
|---|---|---|
| c. Back | Impact or fall on heels or seat | Localized pain over a vertebra, or pain resulting from pressure upon the head. Paralysis of one or more limbs indicates spinal cord damage. |
| d. Rib (see also chest injuries) | Impact or avalanche | Patient has difficulty breathing or coughing due to the pain. Area is painful to the touch and also when chest compression is applied away from the fracture site. |
| e. Pelvis | Impact | Pain on compression. Blood in urine indicates bladder damage. |
| f. Collarbone | Fall — usually on outstretched arm or shoulder | Pain and step-like deformity between shoulder and breastbone. |
| g. Upper arm | Impact, twist, fall | Patient cannot use arm. Look for deformity or protruding bone fragments. |
| h. Lower arm | Fall or twist | Deformity or unusual amount of swelling. |
| i. Thigh (1) Neck of femur | Impact or fall | Common to older persons, in which case a slight fall can cause the fracture. There is some shortening of the whole leg, with the foot turned outward, and with other fracture signs. No swelling; little pain and shock. |

Paralysis indicates extreme emergency and requires prompt transport and proper handling. Keep the patient flat at all times and avoid any forward bending of his body. Roll the patient onto a wide splint such as skis, boards, table top, etc. Put a small pad under the curve of his back to assure a mild hyper-extension. If the Akja or Bergtrage is used, place the patient on his abdomen with rucksack support under chest and thighs. In cases of leg paralysis, give no liquids, as urination may be impossible during transport.

Have the patient exhale, while applying a tight bandage over his lower chest.

Apply tight bandages around the pelvis. If urination is impossible or the urine is bloody, the patient should be transported immediately.

Roll up a shirt or parka, place it across the back of the patient's neck with the ends under the armpits, and tie the ends across the back. If the pain is not too great, use a simple sling with padding under the armpit.

Never use traction, as sharp bone fragments may cut the radial nerve. Using ample padding, immobilize the arm by tying it to the chest. If this position is extremely painful, use splints instead. Never force a fractured arm.

Apply a padded splint the full length of the lower arm. The elbow should be fully flexed and the arm placed in a sling or fastened to the clothing at chest level for support.

Use a long padded splint from the foot to the armpit.

| INJURY | CAUSE | SYMPTOMS |
|---|---|---|
| Fractures (cont.):<br>(2) Shaft of femur | Severe impact or fall | Buckling and swelling of thigh with great shortening of leg; accompanied by great pain and shock. |
| j. Lower leg | Impact, twist, fall | If the inner bone (tibia) is broken, the pain is intense, making walking impossible. However, the patient may be able to walk with a fracture of the thinner outer bone (fibula). |
| Dislocations:<br>1. General directions | Bending of a joint beyond its normal range | Normal contour of the joint is changed. The limb is rigidly fixed (in contrast to a fracture) in an unnatural position. |
| 2. Special types:<br>a. Neck | Impact or fall | The chin points toward one shoulder and is fixed in this position. |
| b. Shoulder | Arm held in a fixed position while body is wrenched, or vice versa | Instead of normal shoulder curvature, there is a hollow spot under the top of the shoulder; the dislocated head of the humerus may be felt below the collarbone inside the top of the shoulder. |
| c. Elbow | Fall on outstretched hand | Prominent protrusion behind elbow, accompanied by swelling. |
| d. Finger, except base of thumb | Overbending | Finger is in rigid bayonet position, accompanied by pain and swelling. Finger is out of line with metacarpal bones. |

The traction splint is best. Otherwise, use a long splint running from below the foot to the armpit. Use Bergtrage frame splinting if no other splints are available. Treat the patient for shock.

Immobilize the leg, with the knee slightly bent. Use plenty of padding over the shinbone; support of the calf is essential to relieve pain. The ideal leg position lines up the gap between the big and second toes with the middle of the knee cap. Never use traction in very cold weather, as permanent damage due to constricted circulation might result. If a splint is unavailable, tie the broken limb to the good limb. If pain is extreme, and only when the temperature is not cold, a traction splint may be used for short hauls. Traction must not be used on long trips, since the boots must be removed to prevent impaired circulation.

Only a physician or properly trained rescuer should attempt reduction. Otherwise, immobilize the patient with well-padded splints in the position most comfortable for him.

Immobilize the neck in a fixed position by supporting the head with clothing placed between head and shoulder. Splint as for neck fracture.

Lay the patient face down on a firm support, let the arm with the dislocated shoulder hang straight down over the edge, then tie a 10- to 15-pound weight to the hand. In 30 to 45 minutes, the muscle spams will relax and the shoulder may reduce itself. If this treatment is unsuccessful, immobilize the shoulder by tying the arm to the chest. If the arm is in a fixed elevated position, then, while providing adequate support, splint the arm in this position.

Tie bent arm to the chest.

Keep a steady pull on the dislocated finger or tip of thumb in a semi-flexed position. At the same time, press the base of the finger toward the fingertip. If this fails, splint the finger as is.

| INJURY | CAUSE | SYMPTOMS |
|--------|-------|----------|
| Dislocations (cont.): e. Base of thumb | Overbending | Swelling with inability to flex whole thumb. |
| Sprained or torn ligaments | Overextension of a joint | Localized pain and swelling, although joint is in correct position. |
| Internal injuries (mainly internal bleeding): 1. General directions | Forceful blow against any body cavity, fall | Gradual failure of circulation indicated by falling body temperature and deathlike pallor. Ensuing physical and mental collapse. |
| 2. Special types: a. Head | Impact or fall | The patient may behave irrationally, even violently, manifesting any degree of disturbed behavior, including deep unconsciousness. He may vomit or have seizures or subsequent paralysis. The pupils may be unequal in size or fail to react to light. There may be blood oozing from ears, nose, or mouth, which indicates skull fracture. The layman may be unable to differentiate between concussion, where there is no bone damage; compression, which involves actual fracture of the skull or damage of the brain by "contrecoup" (brain damage caused by collision with skull unbroken; and brain hemorrhage. Always check for a related neck injury. |

# FIRST AID

Never attempt to reduce the thumb base, as a tendon may be wedged into the joint. This treatment is always a job for a doctor. Immobilize by splinting along thumb, wrist, and forearm.

Immobilize the joint, using a non-elastic bandage and a splint. If in doubt, treat like a fracture. Apply cold packs to the swollen area only if the patient is in a warm, sheltered place. Although taping or the use of elastic bandages may enable the victim to walk out by himself, a far greater damage to the ankle joint limb that is not splinted will be the calculated risk.

Speedy transport of the patient, while preserving the body heat, is paramount. There is little effective first aid outside of a hospital.

1. Check for related neck injury and splint accordingly.
2. Keep air passages open.
3. If there is bleeding, apply a compression bandage around the skull, being extremely careful not to bend the head if damage to neck vertebrae is suspected.
4. Transport the patient immediately to medical care, being as gentle as possible.

185

| INJURY | CAUSE | SYMPTOMS |
|---|---|---|
| Internal injuries (cont.): b. Chest (1) Lungs | Compression; rib fractures piercing the lung; sharp penetration from external object such as ice ax, crampons, or sharp rock | Pain at injured point. Patient may have bluish face and be coughing bright frothy blood. |
| (2) Heart | Blow to front of chest | Fading pulse and extreme bluish discoloration of face. |
| c. Abdomen (1) Bleeding ulcer | Pre-existing condition aggravated by exertion | Patient vomits bright or dark blood (no froth), but usually is not in pain. |
| (2) Ruptured ulcer | Same | Hard abdomen with severe pain as ulcer spills contents of stomach or intestines into abdominal cavity. |
| (3) Bleeding internally from spleen or liver | Impact | Pallor, shock, dull pain in abdomen. |
| d. Kidney, bladder, or ureter | Blow to flanks or lower abdomen | Passage of blood during urination, accompanied by pain between kidneys in back and bladder in front. Sometimes patient is unable to urinate. |
| Exposure to cold: 1. General cooling of body | Temperature drop, moisture, snow, ice, wind, avalanche burial. Contributing factors are hunger, fatigue, or exertion | Three stages: 1. Shivering in an attempt to generate body heat. 2. Apathy, rapid cooling of body, sleepiness, listlessness, indifference. 3. Unconsciousness, glassy stare to the eyes, slow pulse. |

## FIRST AID

The patient may find the prone position intolerable and prefer a half-sitting position. Use a sterile compress, covered by airtight material (such as a plastic or rubber bag) taped to the skin away from the wound, over any chest opening to seal the wound. Place a tight bandage around the lower chest. Transport the patient immediately to a lower altitude so that increased oxygen will ease his breathing.

Transport the patient immediately to medical care, being as gentle as possible.

Transport the patient, with knees flexed, immediately to medical care. Be sure that he receives no food or liquids.

Transport the patient immediately to medical care. Be sure that he receives no food or liquids.

It is essential to keep the patient dry. Replace any wet clothing with dry and use external heat from campfires on both sides of the patient, or hot-water bottles, body heat from rescuers, etc. The patient is unable to generate adequate body heat, so merely placing him in a blanket or a sleeping bag is not a sufficient remedy; however he can be put into a prewarmed sleeping bag if external heat can be used to maintain the warmth level. If the patient is in a warm cabin he may have hot liquids, a warm bath, and a moderate amount of alcohol taken internally if he is not going to be transported further. Smoking should be avoided since it constricts the blood vessels.

187

| INJURY | CAUSE | SYMPTOMS |
|---|---|---|
| Exposure to cold (cont.): 2. Local cooling of body — frostbite or frozen parts of the body | Freezing temperature, tight or inadequate clothing or boots, old age with poor circulation, traction splints applied in freezing weather | Two phases: 1. Superficial: frozen part feels doughy; color is white and does not change to red after pressure is applied. 2. Deep: frozen part is white and feels hard throughout. |
| Snowblindness | Strong sunlight, particularly at higher altitudes. A thin fog layer intensifies snowblindness and sunburn. In altitudes above 12000 feet (4000 m) and in the Arctic and Antarctic, use of amber instead of darker or slit-opening glasses | Eyes water, burn, and feel sandy. There is reddening of the eyelids and the moist covering of the eyes (conjunctiva). |
| Sunburn | Same as snowblindness | Patient's skin is red and painful and may swell (edema) with second degree burn and blisters. |
| Suffocation, including drowning | Obstruction of air passages by snow, sand, food, or liquids | No sign of life, yet no positive indication of death. Patient's face is bluish and his eyes bulge due to lack of air. Pressure on his chest does not move air adequately. In the late stages extreme pallor is evident. |

# FIRST AID

Only the most superficial frostbite may be treated in the field by body heat. The frostbite victim should go immediately to base camp. The affected parts should not be rubbed, chafed, or manipulated in the open. Even if the patient has to walk on a frostbitten limb he should go immediately to base camp. Putting clothing over the frostbite will prevent deepening of the affected area. Once a frostbitten limb has thawed, the patient must be transported on a stretcher. Recent experiences (in Korea and Alaska) indicate that walking even long distances on a frostbitten limb will not lessen the chances of successful treatment if the limb is not thawed out.

After arrival at base camp the conventional method demands gradual warming in water from 42°—46° F (6°—8° C) up to 96°—104° F (36°—40° C) in a period up to 3 hours.

The newer method based on research in Alaska, Korea and by U. S. Navy is as follows: Thaw the frozen area in water ranging from 108°—117° F (42°—45° C) rapidly (for 20 minutes). The dead skin in a frostbitten area must be handled with great care to prevent any infection which would jeopardize recovery.

It is now agreed upon by the "International Medical Conference on Frostbite" at Fairbanks, Alaska; February, 1964, that the ideal temperature for rapidly rewarming is 104° F (40° C).

Cover the patient's eyes completely or have him put on dark glasses. Apply a cold pack moistened with boric acid crystals solutions containing predisolone or hydrocortisone, or eye ointments containing such pain-relieving drugs as pantocaine, etc.

Apply sunburn ointments containing any or all of the following ingredients: hydrocortisone, predisolone, titanium oxide, zinc oxide, bismuth, or paraminobenzoic acid. Do not use tannic acid. The patient should rest and take plenty of liquids. Severe sunburn may cause shock requiring hospitalization.

Remove, as deep as possible, any obstructing materials from the patient's air passages. Remove false teeth. Begin resuscitation using the mouth-to-mouth method; or as second choice, the back-pressure, arm-lift method. The use of a Resusitube will facilitate the mouth-to-mouth method. Give oxygen if available.

| INJURY | CAUSE | SYMPTOMS |
|---|---|---|
| Hanging | Caught in rope | Immediate unconsciousness indicates a fractured second cervical vertebra. Death may be delayed up to ten minutes. |
| Poisoning | Spoiled fresh or canned foods; inedible mushrooms or berries; accidental intake of chemicals or medications | Patient has stomach and intestinal pains, accompanied by vomiting, shock, and unconsciousness ranging to a deep coma. |
| Snakebite | Snakes:<br>(a) Poisonous<br><br>(b) Non-poisonous | (a) Two or four distinct small marks with swelling and increasing pain.<br>(b) Half-circle of fine tooth marks with slight swelling and only moderate pain. |
| Heart attack, complete or partial blockage of coronary arteries, valve malfunction | Recent infection; or heart failure due to advancing age | There is pain in the left side of chest, extending into the left arm. The pulse is weak or irregular and the breath is short. The patient is in pain, accompanied by perspiration and shock. His face is white and his pupils are equally dilated. |
| Apoplexy (stroke) due to thrombosis or hemorrhage inside brain | High blood pressure, often in obese people (may occur at an early age) | Usually one half of the body and face is partially or completely paralyzed. Pain stimulation will not produce a reflex in the paralyzed area. The patient may be in a coma and, whether |

Remove the rope and treat as for a fractured neck, while giving mouth-to-mouth resuscitation.

Induce the patient to vomit by tickling his throat with a feather or finger. Never give an unconscious person food or liquid, as he may suffocate. When the patient regains consciousness, give him water mixed with powdered charcoal (burnt wood), milk, sodium bicarbonate, or soapy water. Keep the patient awake with warm coffee, and transport him to where a proper antidote may be obtained.

Apply a tourniquet between the bite and the heart. Incise the fangmarked area with a sterilized sharp knife or razorblade and let the incision bleed freely. In country inhabited by poisonous snakes, carry a snakebite kit with antisnake serum.

It is essential to transport the patient immediately in a semi-horizontal position, or a position which he finds most comfortable, to medical attention. Give him sedatives or sleeping tablets; if he is in pain, give pain-killing drugs — he himself may carry nitroglycerin tablets.

The patient must be transported immediately in a horizontal position to medical care. If the patient is conscious, he may be given food and liquids.

| INJURY | CAUSE | SYMPTOMS |
|---|---|---|
| Shock Apoplexy (continued) | | conscious or not, is frequently unable to speak. His pupils may be unequal in size and his face may be flushed or bluish. |
| General exhaustion | Inadequate clothing or physical training. Exposure, age, sickness | May range from apathy to unconsciousness. Patient has low temperature, poor pulse, shallow breathing, pallid and haggard face, and may be stumbling and in shock. |
| Mountain sickness | At altitudes above 9000 feet (3000 m), lack of oxygen. Warm winds and humidity aggravate the condition | Fatigue, lack of appetite, indifference, shortness of breath, nausea, vomiting, and dizziness. |
| High-altitude pulmonary edema | Lack of acclimatization | One or two days after reaching 9,000 feet (3,000 m), rather rapidly the patient experiences unusual tiredness, a dry cough, and increasing shortness of breath. Although these symptoms give the impression of a severe pneumonia, they are caused actually by failure of the heart. |
| Sunstroke or heatstroke | Direct exposure of head to sun or heat. High humidity aggravates the condition | The patient is dizzy, tired, thirsty, redfaced, perspiring, and has a racing pulse accompanied by headache. He may go into delirium, with a swift temperature rise to 106° F. |

See that the patient rests, is kept warm, and has dry clothes. Keep his body temperature up, since, as he becomes more exhausted, the less able he is to maintain his own body heat. Put him in a prewarmed sleeping bag and keep up the warmth with fires on both sides of the patient, or from body heat of companions, or hot water bottles, etc. Transport should be delayed until the patient is brought out of shock by means of sugar, liquids, and external heat. The psychological treatment is very important. Employ calmness and determination. It may be necessary to be very forceful to enlist the cooperation of the patient.

Reduce the speed of travel to a regular slow step with a deep breath at each step (rest step). If the patient doesn't improve, a return to lower elevations for acclimatization is mandatory. Failure to do so may precipitate a heart malfunction or exhaustion. Treat the patient for the more serious conditions.

Rapid descent is essential. The patient may have to be carried. Since administration of oxygen would be ideal — if possible order oxygen by ground signal or by radio, to be dropped by helicopter.

Move the patient into the shade, open his clothing, and apply cold packs to his head. While he rests, fan his head and give him cold fruit drinks with salt added. Do not give any beverage containing alcohol.

| INJURY | CAUSE | SYMPTOMS |
|---|---|---|
| Heat exhaustion | Overheating caused by insufficient evaporation, often from inadequate ventilation of non-porous clothing. Usually occurs when air temperature is high | Patient may be unconscious or in a stupor. He is cold, with clammy skin, and has a headache, blurred vision, and muscular cramps. Often he is dizzy and has blurred vision before the attack, which is gradual, with no rise in body temperature. |
| Fainting | Pain, loss of blood, or emotional stress following disturbing scenes | The patient becomes pallid, with cold skin and dilated pupils. He breathes rapidly and is apt to groan before he faints. A fainting person recovers much more quickly after being placed in a horizontal position than does a person who is unconscious from other causes, such as bleeding, shock, or respiratory difficulties. |
| Convulsions | Epilepsy, brain injuries, brain tumors, hysteria. Overdose of insulin in diabetics | The patient may give an initial outcry before violent contractions and thrashings of the limbs and biting of the tongue begin. Parts or all of the body may be affected. Involuntary urinating may occur. There is deep breathing during unconsciousness. |
| Muscle cramps | Overexertion of affected muscles, and insufficient intake of salt and carbohydrates in liquids. (Condition is aggravated by smoking) | Painful contractions in continuous spasms or at intervals. |

194

Place the patient in a horizontal position with his head lower than his feet. Have him rest as much as possible and give him salt in liquid. Note that this treatment is entirely different from heatstroke treatment. In cases of circulatory failfure, give the patient sugar in liquid, and, if possible, digitalis administered by a doctor.

Place the patient in a horizontal position with his head low to restore consciousness. Give him sugar in strong coffee or tea to act as a stimulant and to help restore energy.

Place a bit of soft material between the patient's teeth to prevent him from biting his own tongue and the rescuer's fingers. Pull his tongue forward to ensure unobstructed breathing. If the convulsions occur after a head injury, see the section on head injuries. First check the patient's clothes for drugs prescribed for his condition, then rush him to medical care. If the patient is a known diabetic, give him sugar or orange juice.

Give the patient salt and sugar in liquids, and candy if available. Massage the cramped muscle and apply heat to the cramped area. Move the muscles opposed to the cramped muscle to ease the cramps. Cramps of the chewing muscles of the jaw may indicate lockjaw (tetanus). If there is an infected or dirty wound rush the patient to medical care. (To prevent lockjaw, have a tetanus toxoid booster shot every two years.)

13*

| INJURY | CAUSE | SYMPTOMS |
|---|---|---|
| Nosebleed (epistaxis) | High blood pressure, nose infection, blow on the nose, blowing too hard, scratching on division of nose (septum), overexertion, or exertion at high altitudes | Blood flows from one side of nose. If the blood is flowing from both sides the trouble is low in the throat, or in the stomach or lungs. |
| Death | | The following symptoms, taken together, indicate death. (If they appear singly, some other severe condition exists, but it is highly probable that the patient is still alive.): There may be an odor of decay. The tissue directly under the skin is pale due to lack of blood, while deeper layers show a bluish color due to clotting of blood. Also the body's parts near the ground show bluish discoloration due to the flow by gravity and final clotting of the blood. There is no breath, heartbeat, or pulse. The abdominal wall is rigid. The body temperature is the same as the surrounding environment. The pupils may be dilated or dried up. (If they are contracted — pinpoint size — the patient is still alive.) |

Have the patient lie down and apply an icepack to the bridge of his nose. He should not blow his nose, but nevertheless should spit out blood clots which could run into his stomach and cause vomiting. Pack the bleeding area with gauze or appropriate material to slow the flow so that the blood may clot.

# Bibliography

**Accidents** in North American Mountaineering. **American Alpine Club,** 113, East 90 th Street, New York City, N. Y.: yearly publication, 16 th year.

Symposium on Mouth to Mouth Resuscitation. J. **A. M. A.,** 167, 317—341, May 17, 1958.

First **Aid.** 4 th edition. The **American National Red Cross.** 1957.

Hermann **Angerer.** Hilfeleistung bei Unfällen im Gebirge. Alpenverein, Innsbruck, 1950.

Mountain Operations. Department of the **Army Field Manual,** 31—72, Washington 25, D. C., 1959.

Mountain Search and Rescue in New Zealand, by L. D. **Bridge,** M. B. E. Federated Mountain Clubs of New Zealand, P. O. Box 1604, Wellington. 1961.

Manual of Ski Mountaineering. Edited by David **Brower,** published by the Sierra Club, San Francisco, California, 1962.

Die Klinik und die Behandlung der örtlichen Erfrierungen, by physicians of the Swiss Army: Drs. Hans **Debrunner,** Roman Burri, Rudolf Campell, Walther Jaeger, Arthur Kuoch, Alfred Reist. Med. Verlag Hans Huber, Bern, Switzerland, 1941.

Benjamin G. **Ferris,** Jr., M. D.: Mountain Climbing Accidents in the United States. The New England J. of Med., Vol. 268, No. 8, Febr. 21, 1963, pages 430—431.

Mountain Climbing Safety, The New England J. of Med., Vol. 268, No. 12, pages 662—664.

Mountain Search and Rescue Operations, edited by Ernest K. **Field,** prepared by F. Douglas McLaren, John C. Fonda, Richard M. Emerson, Rangers of Grand Teton National Park and Otto M. Brown, Crater Lake National Park Superintendent, 1960.

Charles S. **Houston,** M. D.: Acute Pulmonary Edema of High Altitude. The New England J. of Med., Vol. 263, No. 10, pages 478—480, Sept. 8, 1960.

**Hultgren,** M. D., Warren B. Spickard, M. D., Kurt Hellriegel, M. D., and Charles S. Houston, M. D.: High Altitude Pulmonary Edema. Medicine, Vol. 40, pages 289—313, 1961.

William R. **Judd,** Irvin E. Hendryson, M. D.: Sitzmarks or Safety? National Ski Patrol System, 1960.

Mountaineering, The Freedom of the Hills. Edited by Harvey **Manning,** published by the Mountaineers, Seattle, Washington, 1962.

William J. **Mills,** Jr., M. D., Robert Whaley, M. D., Winthrop Fish, M. D.: Frostbite: Experience with rapid rewarming, Alaska Med., March 1960, Dec. 1960, June 1961.

A study of frostbite treatment. Naval Research Reviews, March 1962, Washington, D. C.

Dr. Otto **Mock:** Zwölf Jahre Skiarzt über 1000 m, G. Thieme. Leipzig 1936.

**Mountain Rescue,** Cave Rescue. Issued by the Mountain Rescue

Committee of Britain, 1962, Chairman A. S. Pigott. Hill House, Cheadle Hulme, Stockport, Cheshire. This booklet contains a complete list of all rescue organizations and their addresses in Britain.

**Mountain Rescue Unit Instructions.** Montain Club of Kenya. Nairobi 1963.

Mountain Rescues. Helen **Orlob.** Thomas Nelson & Sons, New York, 1963.

Wilhelm **Paulcke.** Nach Emil Zsigmondy: Die Gefahren der Alpen. Munich 1933.

B. **Safar,** M. D. and M. McMahon: Mouth to Airway Emergency Artificial Respiration, J. Am. Med. Ass. 166; 1459—1460, March 22, 1958.

National Ski Patrol System Operational Manual, revised by Charles W. **Schobinger,** National Director. Published 1963. Denver, Colo.

Otto **T. Trott,** M. D., Primary Medical Care for Mountain Accidents in Summer and Winter. Western J. of Surg., Obstetrics and Gynecology, 68: XVIII—XXV; Sept.—Oct. 1960.

Bradford **Washburn:** Frostbite. The Am. Alp. J., Vol. 13, No. 1, issue 36, 1962, pages 1—26.